DESIGNS TO INSPIRE

FROM THE RUDDER 1897–1942

DESIGNS TO INSPIRE

► FROM THE
RUDDER 1897–1942

ANNE and MAYNARD BRAY

 A WOODENBOAT Book

Cover and book design: Lindy Gifford
Printed in the U.S.A.

Published by WoodenBoat Publications
Naskeag Road, PO Box 78
Brooklin, Maine 04616 USA

ISBN: 0-937822-63-9

10 9 8 7 6 5 4 3

CONTENTS

Our purpose in bringing you this book is to celebrate some of the outstanding past efforts in yacht and commercial vessel design. As you might expect, all featured designs are for wooden construction. They range widely in size and type, and some would fit into today's boating environment with few if any changes. Others are too large or impractical. All, however, contain elements worthy of study such as proportions, details, and overall appearance. And all are fine examples of depicting a boat's shape, construction, and arrangement on paper by means of elegant and easily understood drafting. While these works and many others just as good can be dug up by lengthy research, too often the required time and travel prove too inconvenient or expensive. These are renaissance years for classic wooden boats, with lots of restoration, repair, and new construction going on. It is an unbelievable turnaround from, say, 30 years ago. Now, there's a genuine need for more reliable and inspired general information about boats from the first half of the 20th century, and earlier. With this book, we hope to bring the results of our own discoveries to contemporary designers, builders, and owners with the hope that they'll be as inspired, in studying these designs, as we are.

Without *The Rudder*, this book would not be possible. Ceasing publication about 1983, *The Rudder* was the country's first true boating magazine, starting life in 1894. Its editors during the next 50 years started with Thomas Fleming Day who began filling its pages with yacht designer drawings, and ended with Boris Lauer-Leonardi who helped bring L. Francis Herreshoff to guru status. In between, Gerald Taylor White and William F. Crosby stood at *The Rudder*'s helm. The half century beginning with 1894 spans nearly the entire evolution of powerboats and covers the transition from elite yachting to populist yachting in both sail and power. For the sport of recreational boating, it was an amazing 50 years.

The text is intentionally brief because it's the drawings that count here. For more about the gifted designers who depicted these boats, yachts, and vessels, you'll find an annotated appendix. Where known and applicable, the whereabouts of drawing collections is noted as well. *WoodenBoat*'s research library has even more of this kind of information, and soon to be published by W. W. Norton is *An Encyclopedia of Yacht Designers*.

Anne and Maynard Bray
Brooklin, Maine, March 2000

SAILBOATS

CATS

CAPE COD CATBOAT OF 1932
BY FENWICK C. WILLIAMS

LOA   21'0"
Beam   10'0"
Draft   2'6"
Sail Area   342 sq. ft.
Source   September 1932, p. 39

Here's a neat little cruiser by a designer who specialized in catboats and created some real beau-
ties. The cocked-up boom and high seats make for
good visibility from the cockpit, while the peaked-
up gaff assures windward ability. Centerboard
trunks divide the living space in most catboats and
somewhat limit the interior arrangement, but they
come in handy by forming the basic structure for
the drop-leaf cabin table. The enclosed toilet room
is unusual in so small a craft; this one contains a
folding washbasin, linen locker, and shelves.

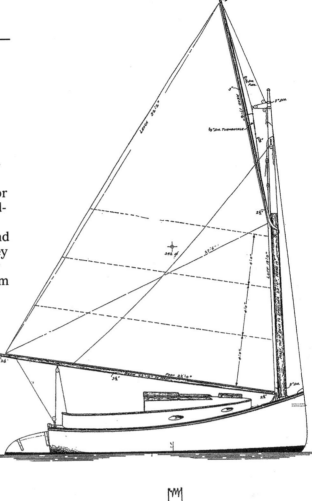

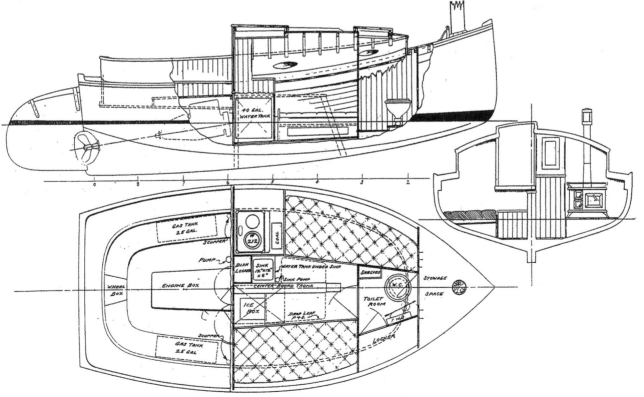

CAPE COD CATBOAT **SEA HOUND** OF 1912 BY CHARLES CROSBY

LOA	25′9″
LWL	25′0″
Beam	11′11″
Draft	2′8″
Sail Area	713 sq. ft.
Source	April 1912, pp. 290-91

You won't heel much in **Sea Hound**, even when it breezes up, because she's so wide. The Crosbys of Osterville, Massachusetts, refined Cape Cod cats as workboats over many years, but created **Sea Hound** for her owner's pleasure rather than for fishing. Crosby experience shows here in elements like the sheered cockpit platform; the handy shelf created by the deck edge as it projects inboard past the cabin sides; and the neat storage bins, drawers, and lockers at the aft end of the cabin. The berths have been inclined in order to better utilize the scant headroom, so you sleep best with your head toward the bow, where it's higher, and your feet aft.

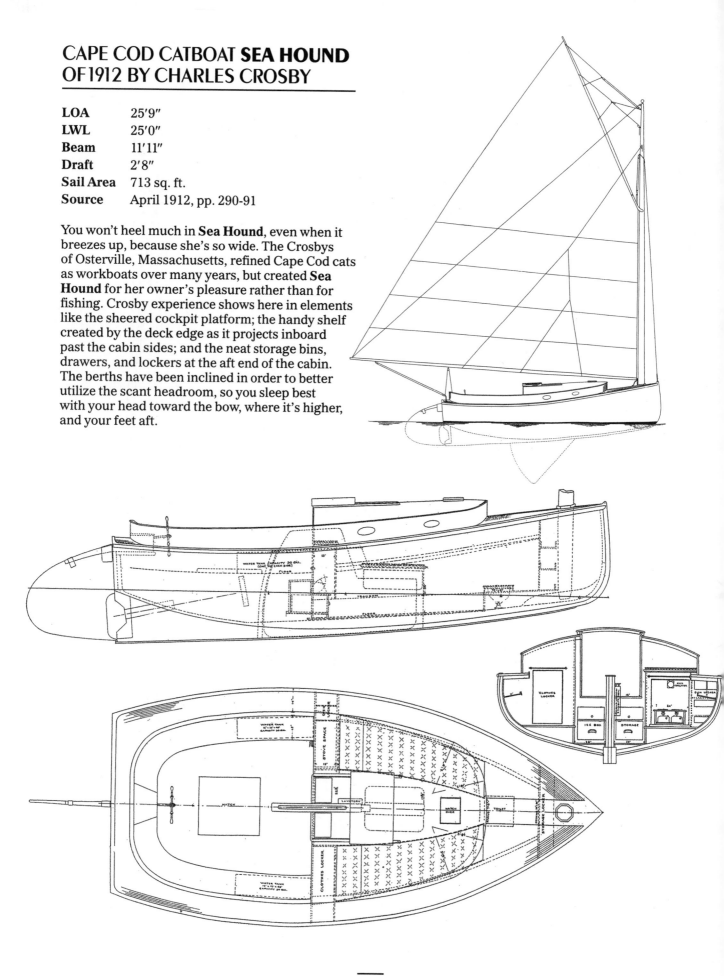

4

CAPE COD CATBOAT MOLLIE II
OF 1931 BY JOHN G. ALDEN

LOA	28'0"
Beam	12'6"
Draft	3'2"
Sail Area	635 sq. ft.
Source	September 1931, p. 56

Enlarging a catboat and proportionally shrinking the length of her cockpit results in great gains in cabin space. There's a private stateroom (meaning one that can be closed off) and a fully enclosed toilet room in this boat in addition to the usual seating and galley. Headroom remains scant, however, being the price paid for a shallow draft hull and a low, handsome profile. The uninterrupted oval shape of the cabin/cockpit when viewed from above greatly enhances a traditional catboat's appearance, and is a device that could be (and sometimes has been) used to advantage on other types of boats. Fittingly, **Mollie II** was built on Cape Cod—by Reuben Bigelow whose Monument Beach shop had turned out the famous ocean racing schooner **Niña** few years earlier.

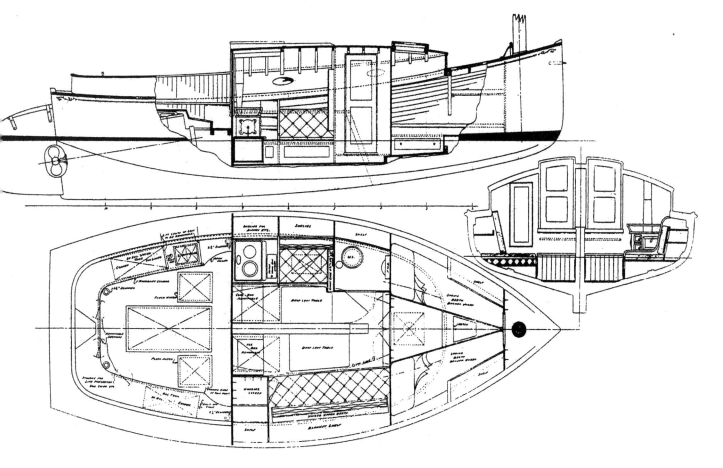

GREAT SOUTH BAY CATBOAT
LUCILE OF 1891 BY GIL SMITH

LOA	21'6"
LWL	17'9"
Beam	7'0"
Draft	1'9"
Sail Area	343 sq. ft.
Source	January 1897, pp. 14-17

Almost as numerous as the Crosby cats of Cape
Cod, Gil Smith's boats emerged with regularity
from his Patchogue, Long Island, shop where they
were designed as well as built. Smith boats are
narrower and built more for speed as recreational
racers for sheltered water than for seaworthiness.
Strip laid decks, natural crook frames, and
wooden rudderstocks prevail here.

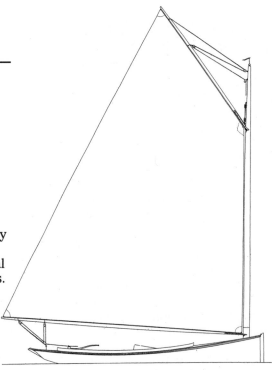

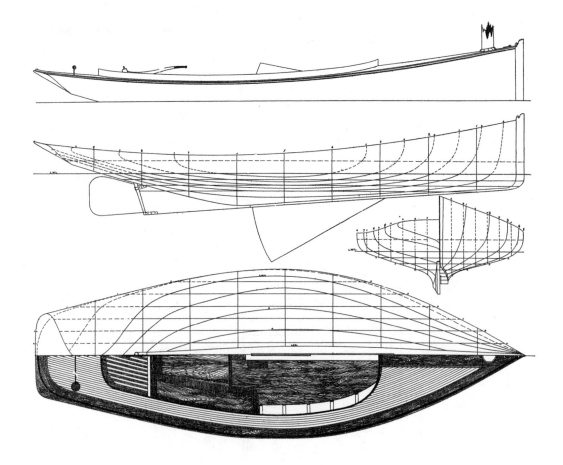

BARNEGAT BAY CATBOAT **SCAT III** OF 1924 BY FRANCIS SWEISGUTH

LOA	33'3"
LWL	28'6"
Beam	12'5"
Draft	2'7"
Sail Area	840 sq. ft.
Source	April 1924, p. 30

Sailors in sheltered New Jersey waters, where racing became a passion, adopted marconi rigs for their catboats. The tall mast required shrouds for support, and the hull near the mast had to be specially reinforced to take the added stress. Owner Edwin J. Schoettle is best known for his comprehensive book *Sailing Craft* published only a few years following **Scat III**'s launching. As editor, Schoettle compiled essays about all the era's popular boat types, including Barnegat Bay catboats, as well as other aspects of yachting.

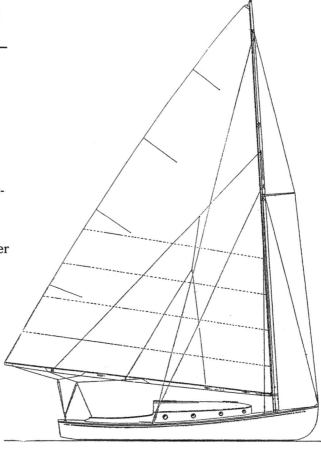

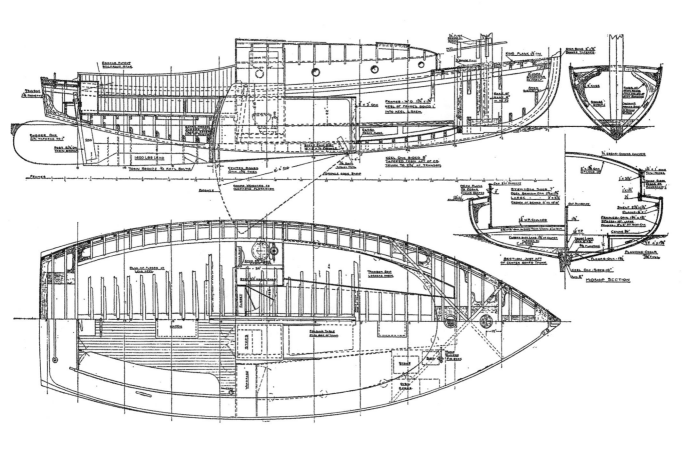

OPEN CATBOAT OF 1906
BY FREDERICK K. LORD

LOA	20′0″
LWL	12′9″
Beam	7′0″
Draft	8″
Sail Area	242 sq. ft.
Source	August 1906, pp. 455-56

Designed to sail in shallow water, this boat has keel and skeg shod with metal for protection against grounding. The oval coaming, curved transom, and overhanging bow and stern make her unusually attractive. Her overhangs are excessive in order to minimize her waterline length. This characteristic as well as her hard bilge and nearly flat bottom were the result of the measurement rule used in this boat's design.

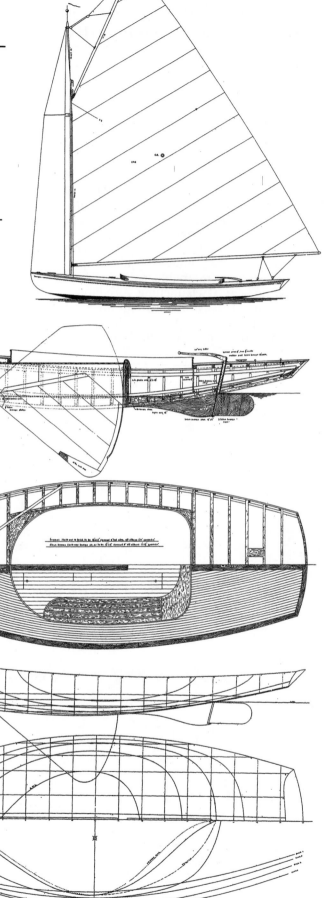

FLYING PROA OF 1898
BY COMMODORE R. M. MUNROE

LOA	30′ 0″
Beam	12′ 4″
Draft	1′ 9″
Source	June 1898, p. 217-220

Proas have to be symmetrical end-to-end because they go one way on one tack and the other way on the opposite tack, with the outrigger always to windward. Here's an easy-to-build proa that, according to her designer, sailed very speedily. None of Commodore Munroe's designs were very deep, as he intended them for shallow Florida waters near Coconut Grove where he was an early settler.

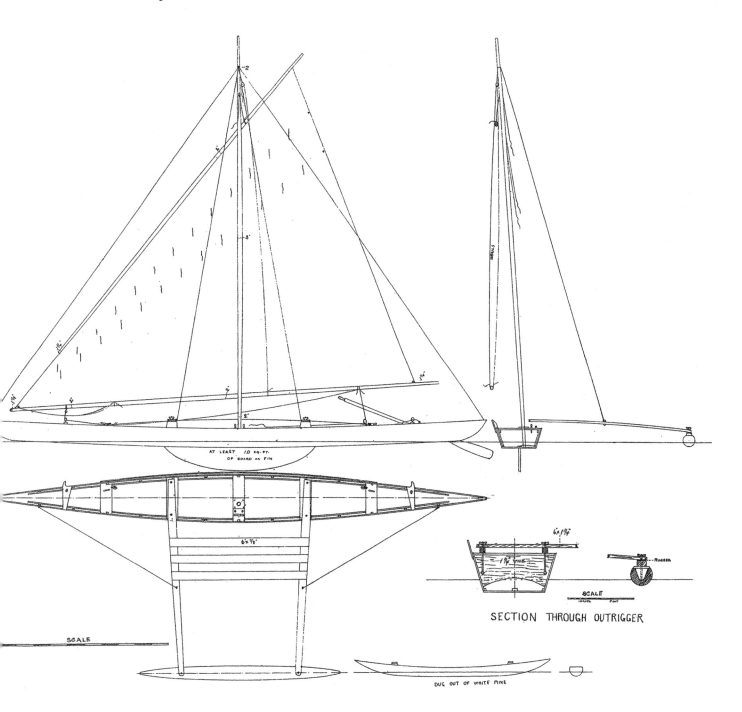

AT LEAST 10 SQ. FT. OF BOARD OR FIN

6″x ⅞″

SCALE

6″x 1¼″

1¼″ THICK

RUDDER

SCALE

SECTION THROUGH OUTRIGGER

DUG OUT OF WHITE PINE

SAILBOATS

SLOOPS

AUXILIARY DORY OF 1924
BY PHILIP L. RHODES

LOA	22'6"
Beam	6'6"
Source	June 1924, p. 28

Fitted with a 3-horsepower engine and a conventional jib-and-gaff-mainsail rig, this partly decked, round-sided, Swampscott-type dory rates highly as a camp cruiser. Nowadays, one of the horizontal, air-cooled, self-contained four-stroke engines might be a better choice than the heavy one-lunger shown here.

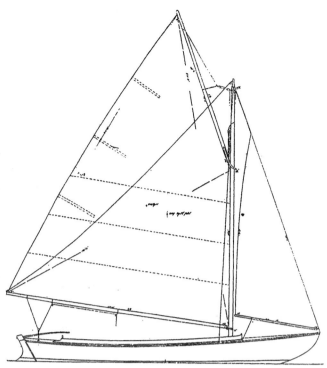

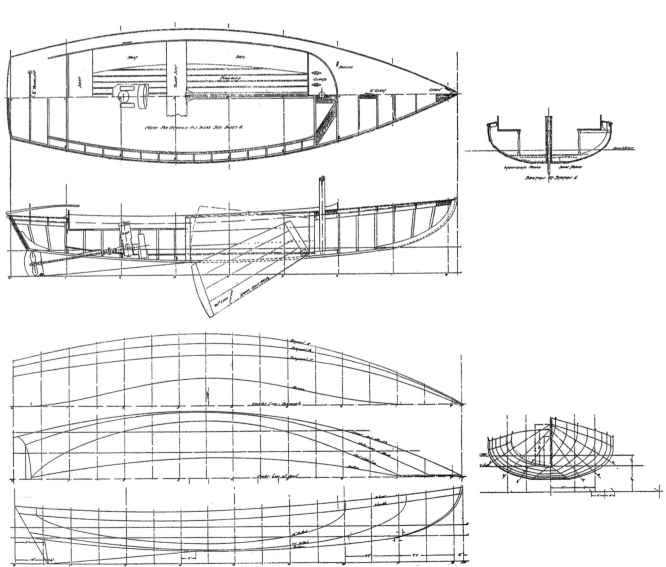

V-BOTTOMED DAYSAILER
RED HEAD OF 1940
BY WILLIAM F. CROSBY

LOA	21'0"
LWL	18'0"
Beam	8'0"
Draft	9"
Sail Area	210 sq. ft.
Source	August 1940, pp. 38-41, September 1940, pp. 30-33, October 1940, pp. 29-32

Designer Crosby was editor of *The Rudder* for many years and ran design after design of his as how-to-build features. Few achieved inspirational status, but his **Red Head** design, shown here, looked great on paper and even better in the flesh. She's big sister to the famous **Snipe**, designed a decade earlier by Crosby, and will accommodate eight in her 6'-by-10' cockpit. Use cedar or other "real wood" for planking, cautions Crosby; sheet plywood won't make it around the hull's compound curves. Complete building plans, beautifully drawn, as well as written instructions are contained in the three-part how-to-build series.

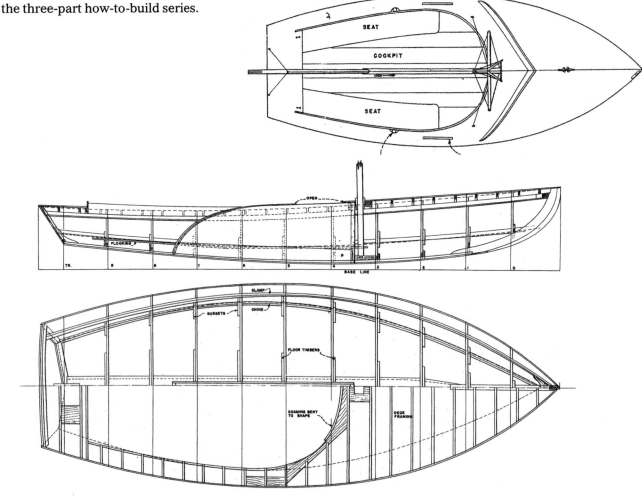

V-BOTTOMED DAYSAILER
OF 1940 BY W. J. SHINN

LOA   14'0"
LWL   12'0"
Beam   5'1"
Sail Area 108 sq. ft.
Source March 1940, p. 44

Proportions weigh heavily in determining both the appearance and performance in any boat, but especially in chine-type hulls because such craft can become boxy-looking if the designer doesn't know what he's doing. That's no problem here, because Mr. Shinn, a New Hampshire shop teacher, had a wonderful eye. Breaking a little from conventional construction, he called for one-piece plywood frames and cedar planking, ⅝" for the topsides and ¾" for the bottom. There's room for four aboard.

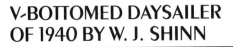

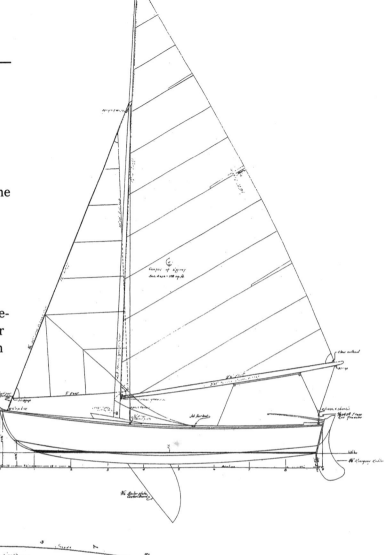
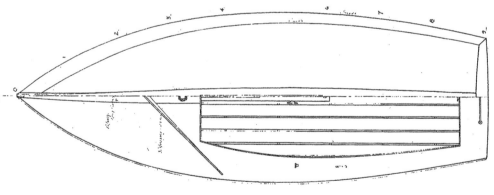
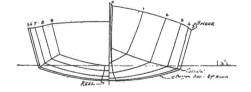
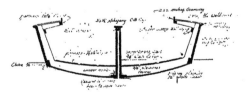

SUICIDE-CLASS SLOOP OF 1934
BY SETH PERSSON

LOA	18'0"
LWL	16'10"
Beam	4'11"
Draft	7"
Sail Area	125 sq. ft.
Displ.	835 lbs.
Source	April 1934, p. 40

A much safer and more enjoyable craft than the class name indicates, boats built to this measurement rule were also known as development boats. The idea was to get the fastest possible craft with 125 square feet of sail area. No two boats were alike, although most were low sided, lightly built, and slippery like this one. Seth Persson, then of Brooklyn, New York, is remembered more as a high-quality builder from Saybrook, Connecticut, than as a designer, although he involved himself in the Suicide class, and an earlier Suicide of his design appeared in the previous year's September issue of *The Rudder*.

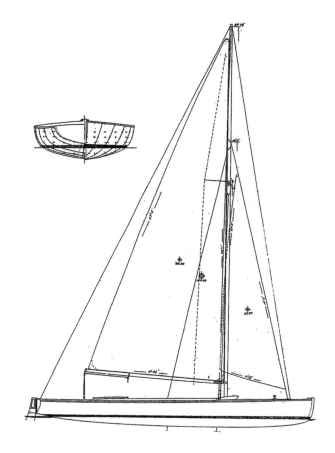

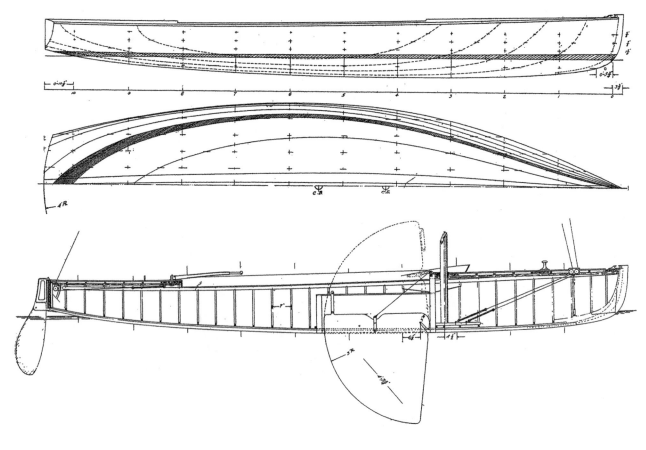

THOUSAND ISLANDS YACHT CLUB ONE-DESIGN SLOOP OF 1912 BY WILLIAM GARDNER

LOA	26′3″
LWL	16′9″
Beam	6′6″
Draft	2′6″
Source	September 1912, pp. 132-34

Most of William Gardner's beautiful creations—including the three-masted schooner **Atlantic,** the America's Cup contender **Vanitie,** and the Larchmont O-class sloops—were much larger than this little gem. Although less well known, this design is no less beautiful. Gardner gave the sheer a slight reverse near the mast—an unusual treatment, skillfully executed. Construction is very light, with ¾″ frames and ½″ planking—same as a Beetle Cat—but in the hands of the Leyere Boat Works of Ogdensburg, New York, the ten boats that comprised the class must have turned out well. With non-ferrous fastenings throughout, these keel/centerboard sloops were built to last. A gunter rig of about these same proportions was used for the early Star-class sloops, another product of this design office. Too bad Gardner's work, except for the few published designs, has gone missing.

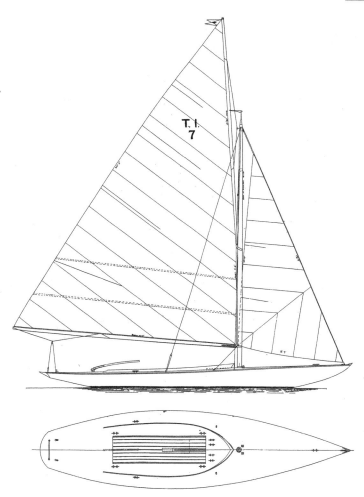

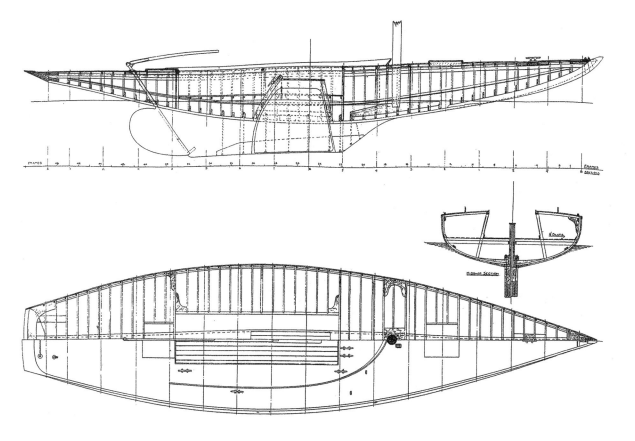

INDIAN HARBOR YACHT CLUB
ONE-DESIGN OF 1916
BY JOHN G. ALDEN

LOA	31′9″
LWL	21′10″
Beam	8′1″
Draft	5′3″
Sail Area	541 sq. ft.
Source	March 1916, pp. 104-5

The slight hollow in the bow above the waterline may be ever so subtle, but it's just this kind of attention to shaping the ends of a hull that produces a craft of unusual beauty. The transom also exhibits just a bit of hollow along its bottom edge. These same features, along with flaring topsides, show up in a number of Alden designs of this era, including the marconi-rigged Triangle-class sloops of Marblehead which came out in the mid-1920s.

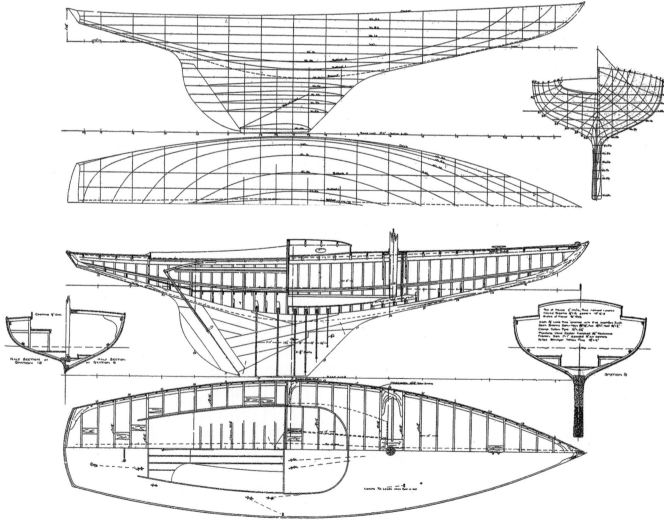

ONE-DESIGN RACEABOUT OF 1900 BY F. S. NOCK

LOA	28'0"
LWL	18'0"
Beam	9'0"
Draft	2'7"
Sail Area	505 sq. ft.
Displ.	3,830 lbs.
Source	February 1902, pp. 47-49

In spite of their low freeboard, these raceabouts proved seaworthy on their maiden passage home to Pawtuxet, Rhode Island, from eastern Connecticut (where they were built by the Holmes Shipbuilding Co. of Mystic), beating into the teeth of a brisk easterly wind and high seas. The well-rounded forward sections must have kept them from pounding. Leaking centerboard trunks—a notorious Achilles' heel in most keel/centerboarders—won't be a problem for these craft, since the centerboard is housed entirely within the fin beneath the timber keel.

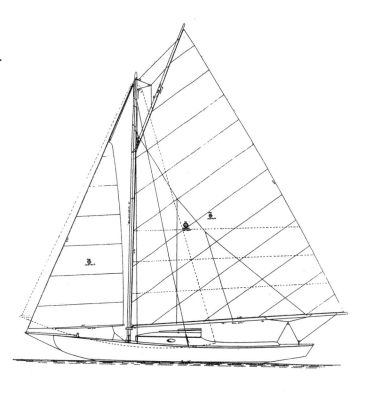

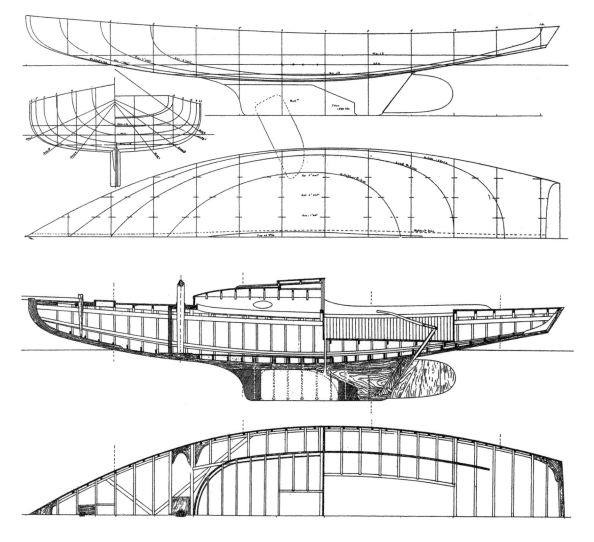

INDIAN HARBOR YACHT CLUB
R-CLASS SLOOP OF 1914
BY FREDERICK W. GOELLER

LOA	35'9"
LWL	21'1"
Beam	7'9"
Draft	5'1"
Source	July 1914, pp. 357-58

Although there is no lines drawing extant that we know of, a good draftsman could come pretty close to duplicating the hull shape by making use of the profile, half-breadth, and sections published here. This is smaller than the usual R-boat, being shorter on the waterline by several feet and having about a foot less draft. But what a handsome craft! If building her today, a marconi rig and perhaps a plywood deck would be worth considering.

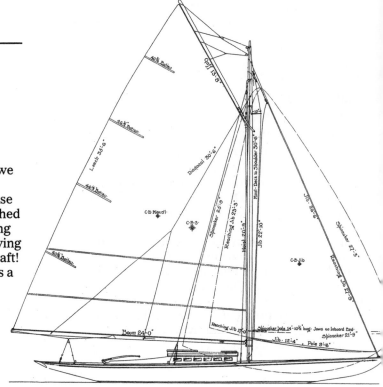

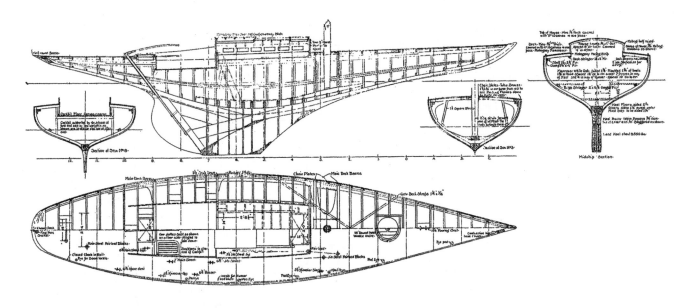

GAFF CRUISING SLOOP AIMEE
OF 1906 BY JOHN G. ALDEN

LOA	33'7"
LWL	25'0"
Beam	11'0"
Draft	5'6"
Sail Area	709 sq. ft. (working sails)
Source	January 1906, p. 28 & 29

Working craft frequently evolve into graceful shapes and proportions while, at the same time, being able to fulfill their primary function. Designer Alden often seized upon a workboat type as the basis for his designs, this early one coming from the fishing sloops of Gloucester, Massachusetts. Plenty of beam, a strong sheer, and hard bilges make her handsome indeed. But even below deck, the fishing boat tradition carries on: her arrangement is much like a fishing vessel's fo'c's'le with pilot berths out against the hull and settees inboard of them where the crew can sit, eat, or lounge. My only desire would be for a round-fronted trunk cabin instead of the flat one shown.

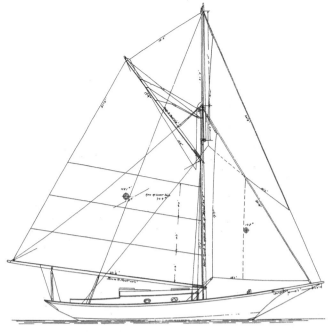

Although the magazine mentions a Mr. Brown of Pulpit Harbor (on North Haven, Maine) as the builder, *Lloyd's Register* confirms that **Aimee** was actually a product of Wilbur Morse's Friendship, Maine, shop. It's not hard to recognize a little of the Friendship sloop in her shapely hull.

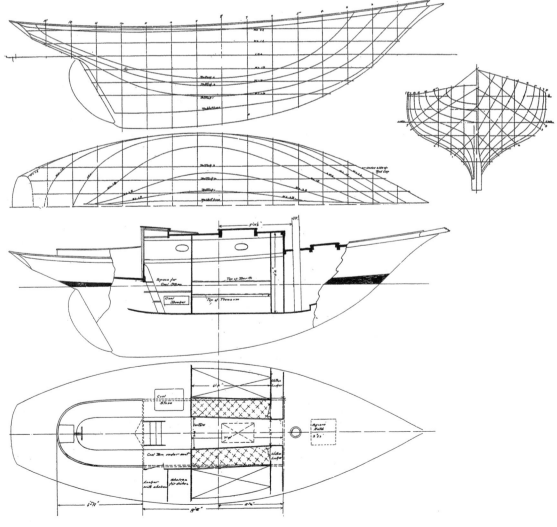

GAFF CRUISING SLOOP
OF 1904 BY E. A. BOARDMAN

LOA	48'10"
LWL	30'0"
Beam	12'0"
Draft	7'0"
Sail Area	1,300 sq. ft.
Source	March 1905, pp. 118-20

Discovering published plans, sufficient to build from, for a yacht of this size is a rare treat. But when the depicted craft is well-nigh perfect, you feel even luckier. The hull would be set up on the wide-spaced sawn frames that show in the drawings, and after planking the intermediate frames would be steamed, sprung into place, and fastened. The drawings are so detailed that even the towels, pillows, and books have been provided for. On a cruise, the cabin flooded with sunlight streaming in through the overhead skylight, with those long settees and the dining table set for the noonday meal, would tempt one to abandon the helm and step below.

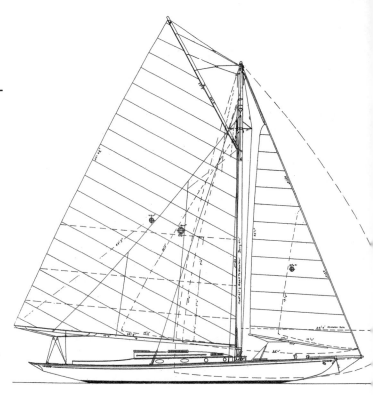

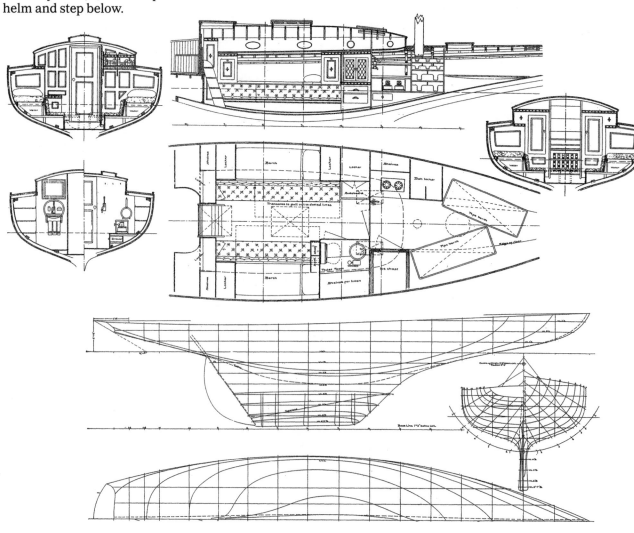

KEEL/CENTERBOARD CRUISER OF 1914 BY COX & STEVENS

LOA	42'3"
LWL	26'8"
Beam	10'9"
Draft	4'0"
Source	April 1914, pp. 223-24

Among the hundreds of designs this prolific firm turned out, I've never seen a dud. And the drawings are consistently as well crafted as the boats depicted on them. This shallow cruiser is a perfect example; I only wish the lines and other supporting drawings had been published. She's a little shy on headroom—the price of a low profile and 4' draft—but the designers have sprung down the cabin sole to get all possible height above it and have kept the centerboard trunk out of sight as well. I especially like her profile and the oval shapes of her cabin and coaming when viewed from above.

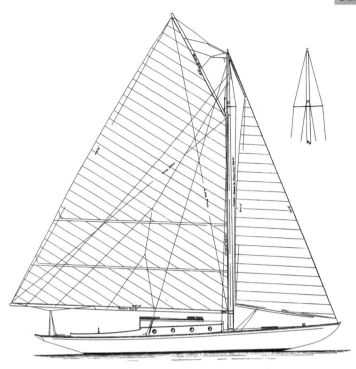

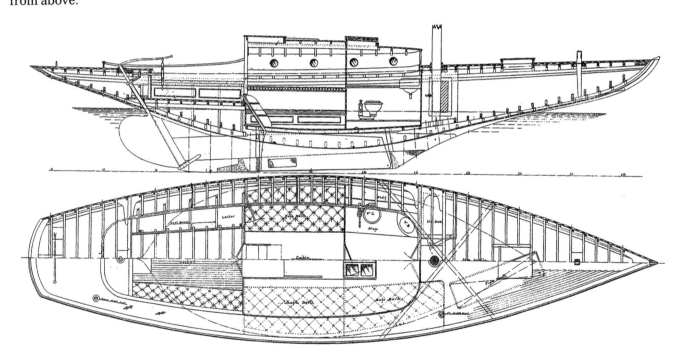

GAFF SLOOP **DYON** OF 1924
BY LUDERS & SMITH

LOA	51'0"
LWL	35'10"
Beam	13'0"
Draft	7'6"
Source	July 1925, p. 25

Dyon is one of the few sailing yachts that A. E. Luders, Sr. put his hand to, as most of his considerable talent was directed to power craft. **Dyon** is also one of the few sailing yachts of her size that has never been restored and still is as she was when new: gaff rig, varnished cabintop, chain-driven propeller shaft. Even the cast bronze miniature hawk (from which her name derives) still adorns the stemhead. No sheet or halyard winches have ever been installed. P. L. Smith, for whom **Dyon** was built, claims credit as co-designer in *Lloyd's Register*, even though there's no mention of this collaboration in *The Rudder*. **Dyon** is still a Smith family treasure, four generations and three-quarters of a century later, and still sails from Tenants Harbor, Maine. You can learn more about this remarkable yacht in *WoodenBoat* No. 64.

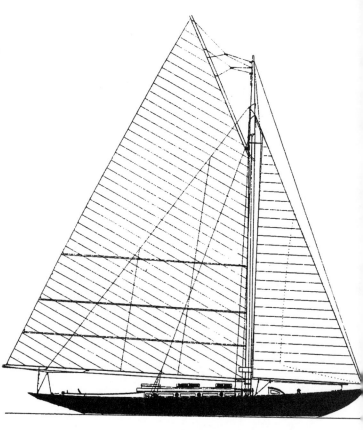

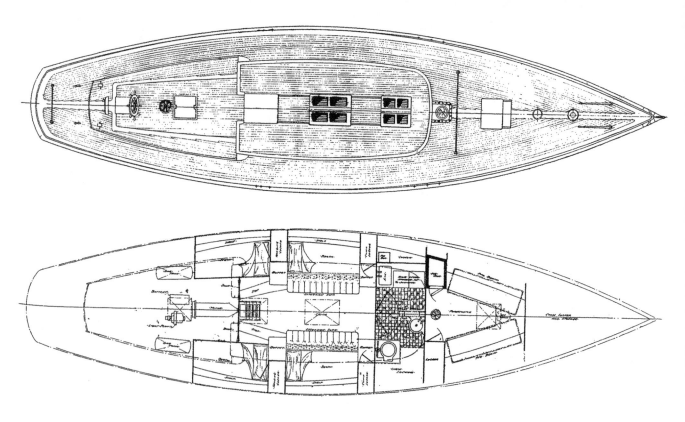

CRUISING SLOOP **WINDWARD**
OF 1928 BY PHILIP L. RHODES

LOA	35′5″
LWL	25′0″
Beam	9′6″
Draft	5′0″
Sail Area	636 sq. ft.
Source	July 1928, pp. 46-47

M. M. Davis of Solomons, Maryland, built **Windward** for Aubrey King of Baltimore. She's quite lovely, as are most of Rhodes's boats, and her lively sheer and slightly hollow transom profile are in part responsible. The rig looks like a bit of a handful, with two headsails and running backstays, so increasing the mast height, shortening the boom for a standing backstay, and getting more luff length in a single jib might make sense. Below, the reviewer for *The Rudder* criticized the lack of hanging lockers. In forgoing them, however, Rhodes has achieved a symmetrical and most pleasant interior that can sleep four. To maintain this uncluttered ambiance, using seabags for clothes would be a small inconvenience.

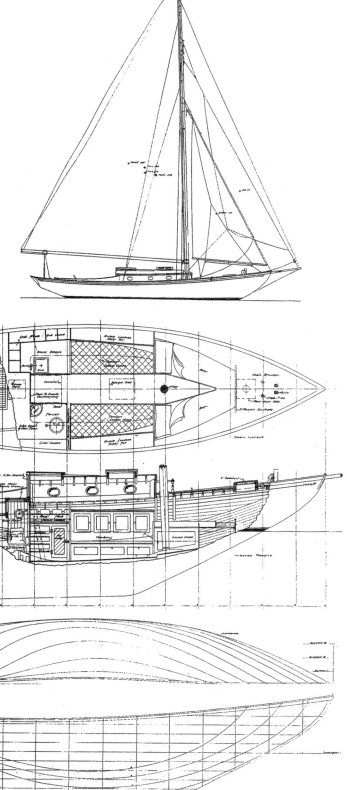

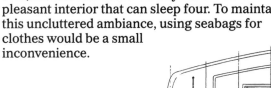

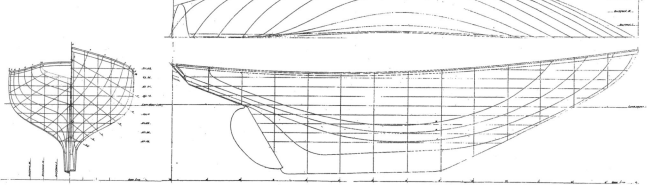

MODERN FRIENDSHIP SLOOP OF 1931 BY RALPH E. WINSLOW

LOA	31'7"
LWL	24'11"
Beam	10'4"
Draft	5'2"
Sail Area	648 sq. ft.
Displ.	17,650 lbs.
Sources	March 1931, pp. 69-75 (a complete how-to-build article); June 1933, p. 36 (for an alternate yawl rig); May 1941, pp. 38-39 (for a slightly smaller, but similar design with a ketch rig, this time with the enclosed head on the port side as it should be)

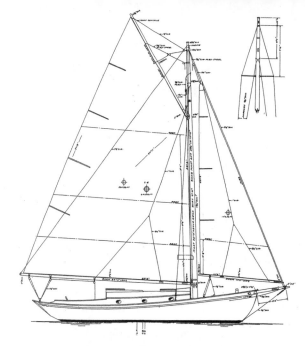

By softening the bilges, reducing the keel drag, yet retaining the lovely and characteristic rolled-in quarters and giving her a full-length iron ballast keel, designer Winslow has made the Maine Friendship sloop over into a practical cruiser. He even offered alternate ketch and yawl rigs in subsequent issues of *The Rudder*, and has included a marconi sloop sail plan along with the gaff sloop rig shown initially. The interior has the galley and enclosed head aft with a symmetrical, four-berth layout running forward from there.

In keeping with the economy-minded sailors of the Depression era, Winslow called for galvanized steel fastenings which make little sense today, given the high cost of labor and the small difference in price of fastening materials; bronze screws and bolts would be the way to go now. For protection against grounding, that stiff cast-iron ballast keel still seems like a good idea, but fastened with Monel in lieu of galvanized bolts. One might also want to consider a plywood deck sheathed with Dynel and epoxy; it would not only be quicker to install, but will withstand neglect far better than the laid and caulked deck called for in the drawings.

Ralph Winslow's time spent in the Herreshoff Mfg. Co.'s drafting room (he worked there during and after WWI) shows in these and most of his other plans. Square-sectioned frames, for example, laid exactly parallel to each other are a HMCo. characteristic, as is the beveling of their outboard faces to take the planking. Dig out the three articles if this boat interests you; they are filled with good detail including written specifications.

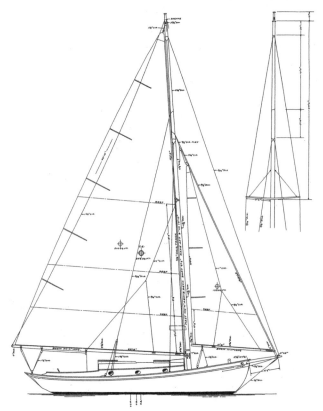

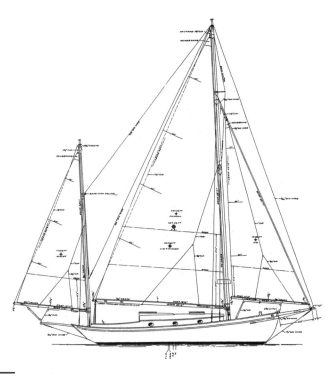

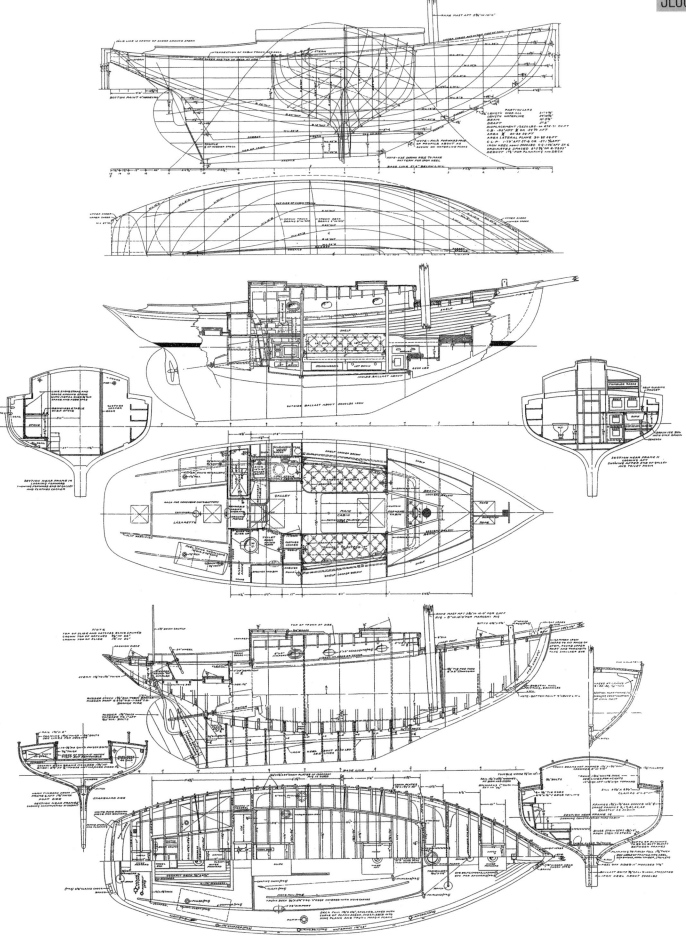

PLUMB-STEMMED CUTTER
ROARING BESSIE
OF 1933 BY S. S. CROCKER

LOA	30'3"
LWL	28'7"
Beam	10'9"
Draft	4'9"
Source	January 1933, p. 40

Built in Swampscott, Massachusetts, by George Chaisson and owned for many years by Burnham Porter, who also resided on the north shore, **Roaring Bessie** inspired a series of nearly identical Amantha cutters turned out by Palmer Scott's Fairhaven yard near the head of Buzzards Bay. The Amanthas carried marconi rigs, and eventually so did **Bessie.** Plumb stems (and the hollow bow that results), strong sheers, and an overall shippy appearance are Crocker trademarks. **Roaring Bessie** looks friendly, and indeed she was, as the many who were invited aboard can attest. Enjoying a glass of Mount Gay rum below while leaning back, absorbing the ambiance, and listening to owner Porter talk about his pride and joy was an experience not soon forgotten.

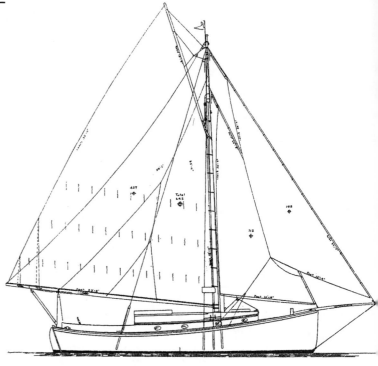

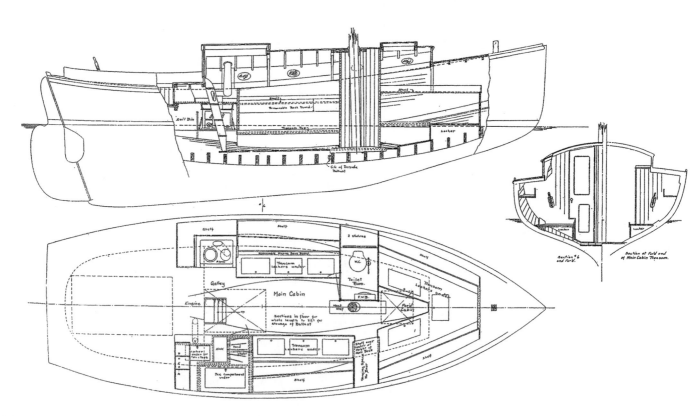

POCKET CRUISING SLOOP
CHANTEY OF 1929
BY PHILIP L. RHODES

LOA 23′0″
LWL 17′6″
Beam 7′3″
Draft 3′1″
Sail Area 300 sq. ft.
Source August 1929, pp. 54-55

"Perhaps the most interesting [design] ever published of a boat of so small a length," stated *The Rudder*. These words may be a bit of a stretch, but are still quite a tribute. **Chantey** was well built by Henry B. Nevins, Inc., one of the nation's premier yacht yards. Her construction plan shows a sprung keel timber and a centerboard trunk that is contained entirely beneath the cabin sole. The mahogany-planked hull is strapped diagonally in way of the mast, and the drawings are so detailed that even the built-in bilge pump is depicted. She's cramped below deck—as are most 23-footers—but there are two nice berths and a place for a small galley forward near the mast. Too bad her long boom precludes using a permanent backstay between the masthead and the transom, but tending the runners she's fitted with wouldn't be too troublesome; they're all that needs tending when coming about. The jib and mainsail sheets can be left alone during a tack.

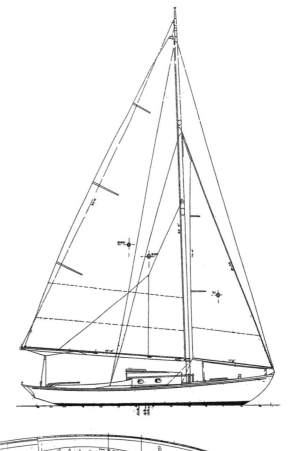

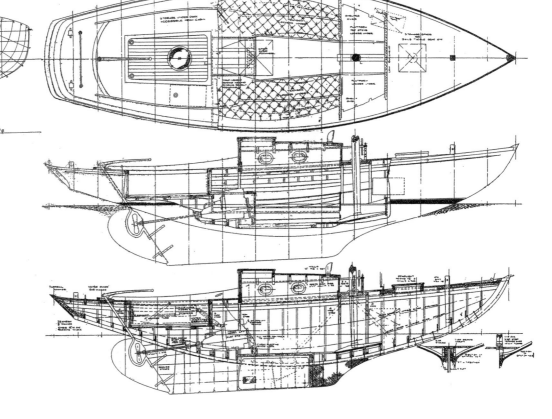

GAFF CRUISING SLOOP OF 1933
BY FENWICK C. WILLIAMS

LOA	30′0″
LWL	23′5″
Beam	9′0″
Draft	4′9″
Sail Area	448 sq. ft.
Source	June 1933, p. 39

A full forebody and a long run, sometimes described as a cod's head and mackerel's tail, while not carried to excess here, nevertheless have been moderately applied in this boat's lines drawing. It's one way of increasing the interior space near the mast, as is the relatively high freeboard forward. High bows with low sterns like this enhance the appearance of most boats, and rolled-in quarters that allow an elliptical transom outline help as well. All in all, it's a fine design, with the possible exception of the cabin arrangement where the toilet room seems to occupy prime space, leaving the galley crammed adjacent to the mast beyond the perimeter of the trunk cabin.

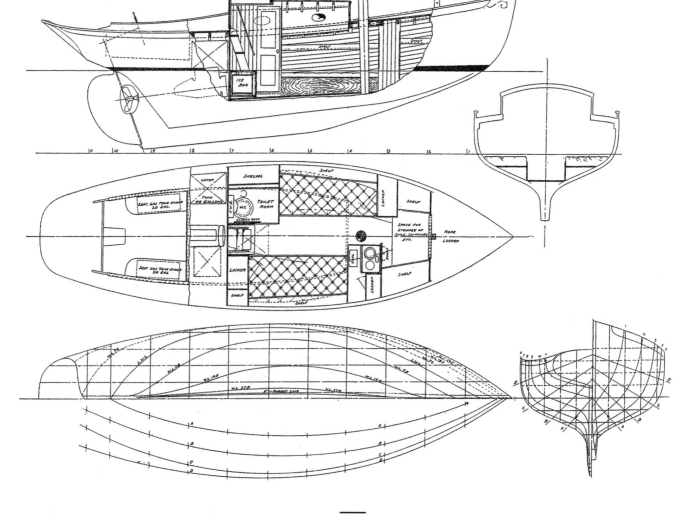

CRUISING SLOOP **BALTICA**
OF 1937 BY K. AAGE NIELSEN

LOA	38′6″
LWL	29′0″
Beam	10′1″
Draft	5′5″
Sail Area	612 sq. ft.
Displ.	16,800 lbs.
Source	May 1935, p. 41 and
	December 1937, p. 46

Aage Nielsen first prepared these drawings for a design competition while he was associated with Murray Peterson (and shortly after both men left the John Alden office). The Swedish Cruising Club bought this design, but a couple of years later Nielsen came up with a nearly identical one, also named **Baltica**. By then, he was serving as the Boston branch of Sparkman & Stephens. The client for the second **Baltica** was C. T. Crocker III; Palmer Scott of Fairhaven, Massachusetts, was the builder. Nielsen gave the second **Baltica** slightly more freeboard, a longer cabin, less rake to the mast, and a little more sail area. Below deck, however, the two designs differ considerably, even though they both sleep four. In later years, Aage Nielsen became secretive and held back lines drawings from publication, so it's a real treat to

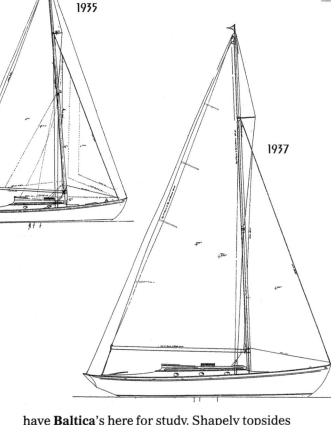

have **Baltica**'s here for study. Shapely topsides with not a trace of wall-sidedness, and a sheer that sweeps up more than most at the bow and stern are but two features this skillful designer incorporated into both versions of **Baltica**.

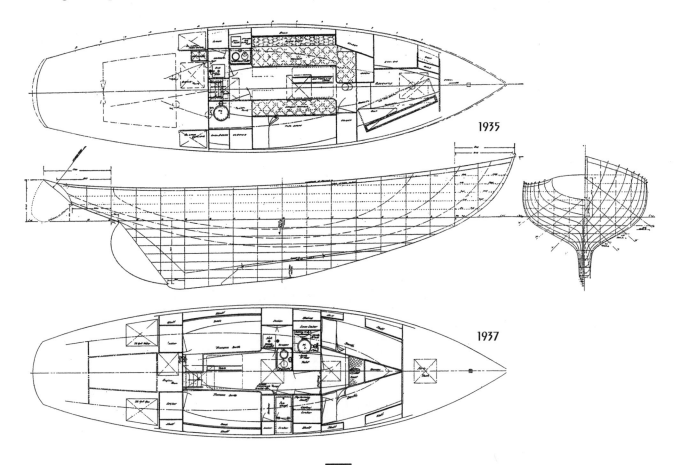

CRUISING SLOOP **PENRITH** OF 1935 BY SPARKMAN & STEPHENS

LOA	43'11"
LWL	32'0"
Beam	10'11"
Draft	5'11"
Sail Area	934 sq. ft.
Displ.	25,350 lbs.
Source	June 1935, p. 47

By the mid-1930s when **Penrith** was designed, the office of Sparkman & Stephens had established a handsome and recognizable profile for its sailing yachts: a pleasing sheer, a long, low trunk cabin, a moderate rig with permanent backstay, and (for publication) the hull in the sail plan was always done in black. **Penrith** appears to have been built by her owner John M. Nelson, The Nelson Corporation being the builder of record. I especially like the seating below deck where not only the usual main cabin berth/settees are available, but the adjoining quarter berths as well, since they are at the same level. (The usual practice is to raise quarter berths so they can be wider.) Out of **Penrith**'s design evolved the famous New York 32s, a year later from the same office—those boats being only slightly longer, and a little narrower and deeper.

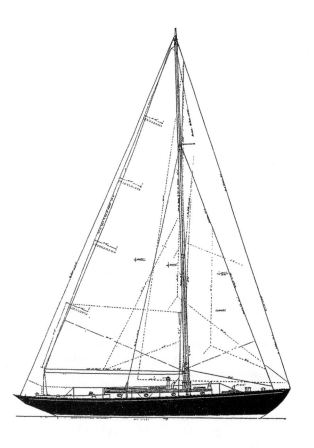

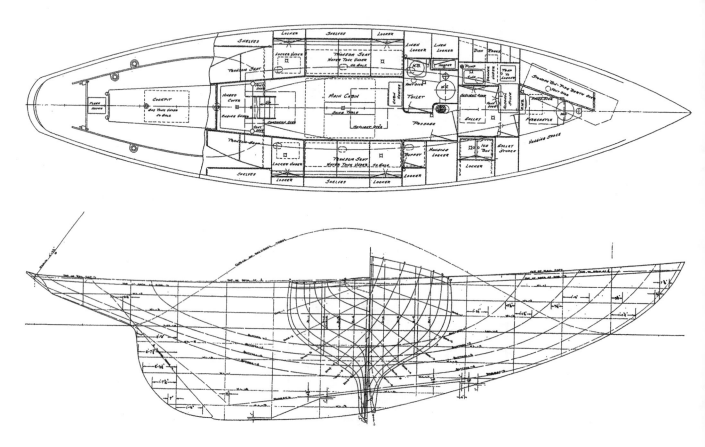

CRUISING/RACING SLOOP OF 1935 BY HENRY J. GIELOW

LOA	38′0″
LWL	26′8″
Beam	9′6″
Draft	5′6″
Sail Area	650 sq. ft.
Source	March 1935, p. 62

Like Cox & Stevens, the Gielow firm specialized in large and lovely yachts and vessels. But when either firm dropped down to smaller craft, the result was just as noteworthy. This boat, for example, merits a close look. Besides the pleasing profile, it's interesting to see what the designers have done with the main cabin settees. In a boat with only a 9′6″ beam there's no possibility of pilot berths, so they've mounted the upper berths in two different sets of supports so they can serve as berths at night and seat backs by day. Thus, six can sleep aboard. Otherwise, the interior, in soothing symmetry, represents pretty much the standard layout for a cruising auxiliary in the 40′ range: galley aft; a main cabin for eating, sitting, and sleep-

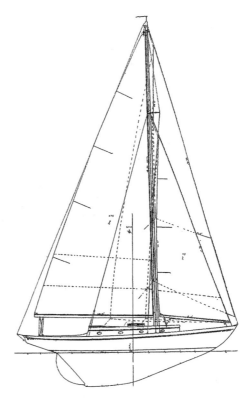

ing; an enclosed head to port near the mast with hanging lockers opposite; and a pair of berths forward. It's a setup that has proven hard to beat.

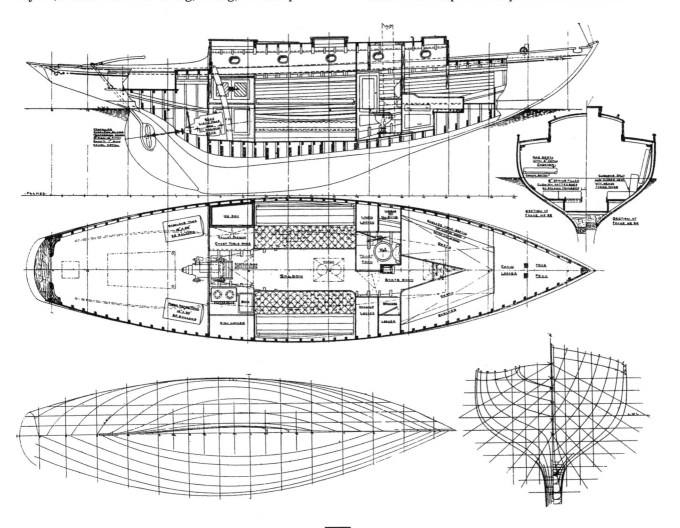

CRUISING SLOOP **STORM SIGNAL**
OF 1935 BY J. ARTHUR STEVENS

LOA	28′0″
LWL	22′0″
Beam	8′6″
Draft	4′6″
Source	January 1935, p. 42

By making the trunk cabin high with lots of crown, designer Stevens has been able to achieve headroom of 5′8″, a generous amount for so small and shallow a boat, and he's accomplished this without ruining the looks. Keeping the cabin narrow and giving the hull a high bow and strong sheer help avoid boxiness. This was to be a stock offering of Goudy & Stevens of East Boothbay, Maine, a boatyard in which the designer was a partner.

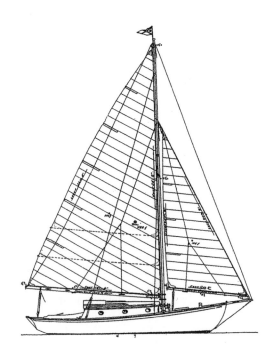

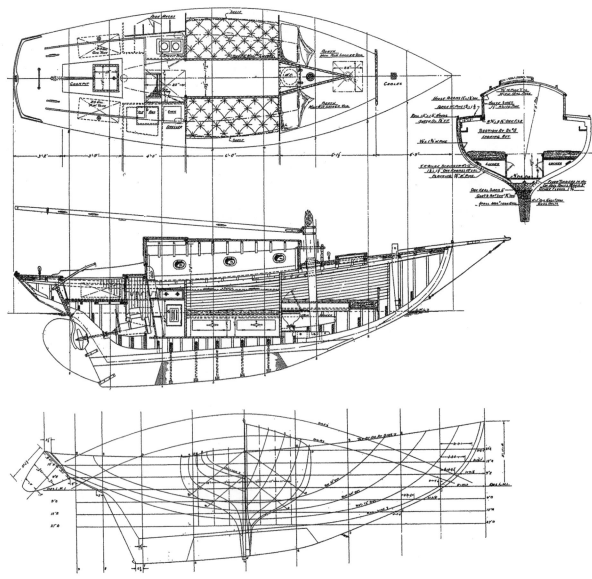

SHORT-ENDED CRUISER OF 1934 BY WINTHROP L. WARNER

LOA	25′9″
LWL	22′8″
Beam	9′1″
Draft	4′5″
Sail Area	502 sq. ft.
Displ.	12,400 lbs.
Source	October 1934, p. 44

A cut above the ordinary, with the embellishments Warner loved to draw, this is a little ship and complete with sprung-down bowsprit and boomkin, inset bulwark, curved transom, laid decks, boom gallows, and, of course, a covestripe terminating with scrolls at each end. Below deck, seating is tight, but otherwise the accommodations are first rate for two persons. Alternate arrangements were drawn and can be obtained from Mystic Seaport where the Warner collection resides.

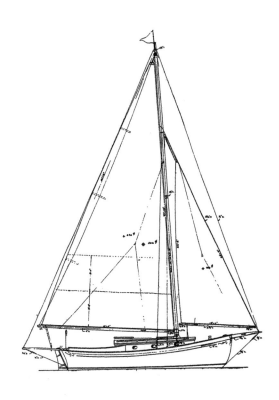

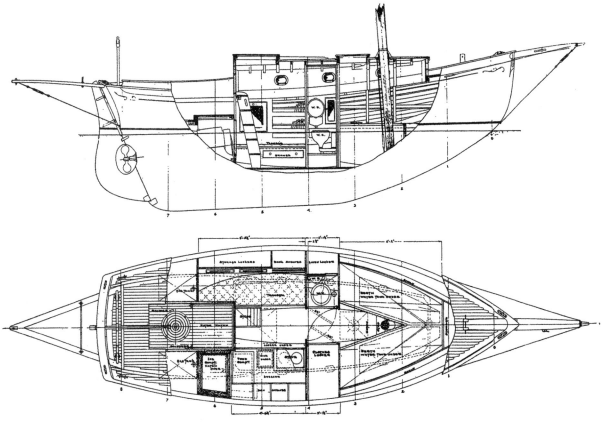

RAISED-DECK CRUISER
OF 1936 BY JOHN G. ALDEN

LOA	28'2"
LWL	21'5"
Beam	8'6"
Draft	4'7"
Sail Area	384 sq. ft.
Source	June 1936, p. 50

Because this boat's raised deck is confined to the 'midships third of her length and doesn't extend forward to the stem, she appears more graceful than others of her type. Below, the cabin is unusually spacious. Here, the running backstays serve only to keep the jibstay tight, since their traditional role of holding back the mast has been taken over by the permanent, or preventer, backstay. This was to be a stock offering of Milton Boat Yard of Rye, New York.

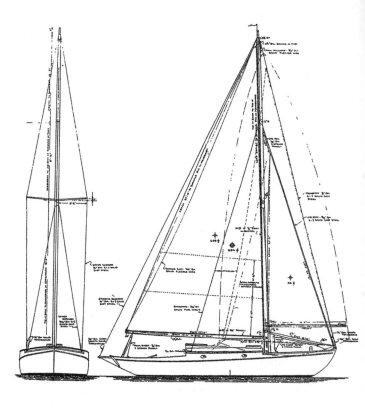

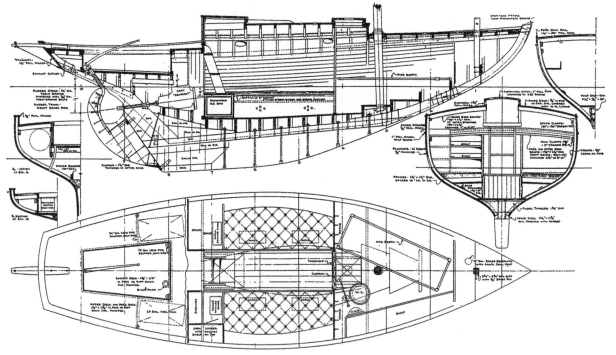

CRUISING SLOOP **LITTLE SISTER**
OF 1938 BY PHILIP L. RHODES

LOA	27'2"
LWL	22'1"
Beam	8'3"
Draft	4'2"
Sail Area	350 sq. ft.
Source	May. 1938, p. 39

The doghouse provides full headroom in the galley where standing is preferable to sitting, and rather than hurting this boat's looks, the doghouse actually makes her distinctive. Two people are accommodated easily with plenty of storage space left over in the forepeak as well as around the engine. Gray Boats of Thomaston, Maine, built several **Little Sisters** as standardized cruisers.

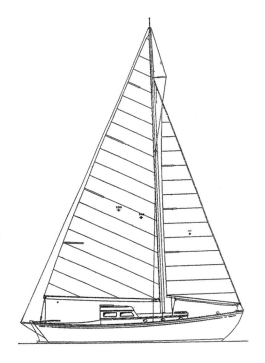

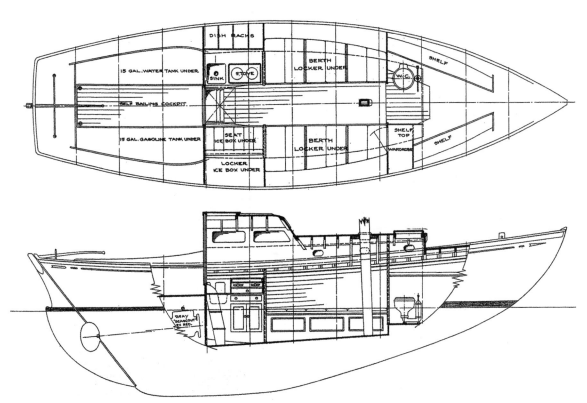

CONCORDIA 25 CRUISING SLOOP OF 1942 BY CONCORDIA CO.

LOA	31'3"
LWL	25'4"
Beam	9'4"
Draft	5'1"
Sail Area	538 sq. ft.
Disp.	14,270 lbs.
Source	August 1942, p. 33-35

By stretching the hull only about 3' and making it a little deeper than Rhodes's **Little Sister** (page 35), you can fit in comfortable accommodations for four and have full headroom throughout. As practical family cruisers, these boats (later known as Concordia 31s) became well respected. Like their larger sisters, the well-known Concordia yawls, they featured fold-down backrest/berths and knotty pine interiors—just the kind of cabin that welcomes you below after a day of sailing.

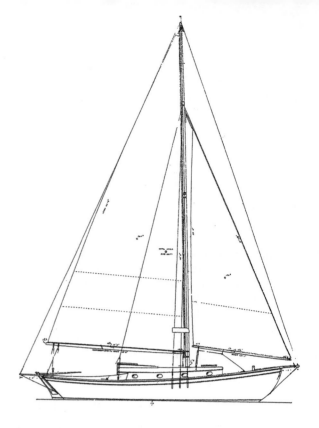

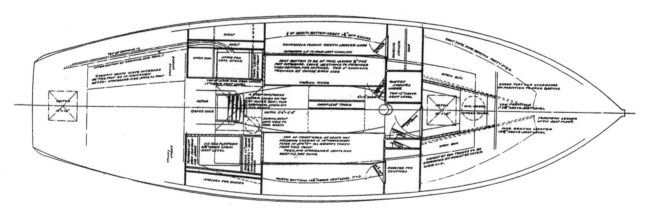

D-39 DOGHOUSE SLOOP
OF 1940 BY GILBERT DUNHAM

LOA	38'11"
LWL	28'9"
Beam	10'0"
Draft	5'11"
Sail Area	677 sq. ft.
Source	February 1940, p. 39

Gil Dunham's interior drawings are so realistic that anyone can understand them. Innovative arrangements below deck were another of his traits and show up here as the novel hinged seats within the doghouse and the sliding hatch over the engine. Boats like this, because of their two head-sails, are sometimes known as cutters rather than sloops. True cutters, however, have other distinguishing features such as a narrow beam and deeper-than-normal draft. Regardless of semantics, having two headsails instead of one allows more ways to reduce sail when the wind pipes up.

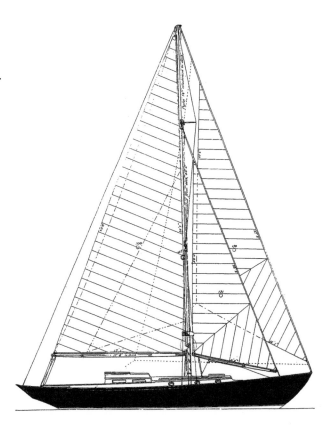

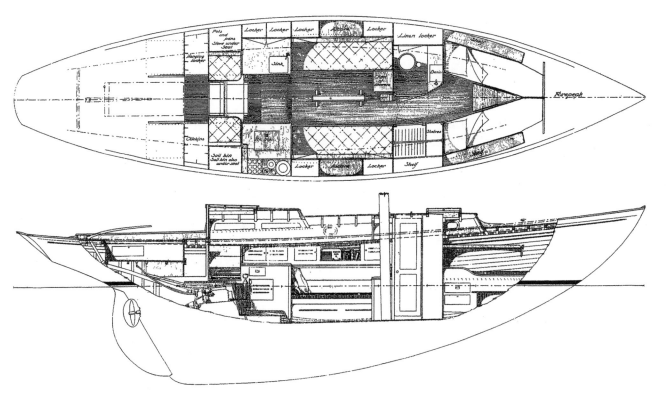

CUTTER **NANCY LLOYD** OF 1938
BY PHILIP L. RHODES

LOA	47'0"
LWL	34'0"
Beam	11'8"
Draft	4'6"
Sail Area	911 sq. ft.
Source	October 1938, p. 38

Here's another interior that's out of the ordinary: a double bed forward, a desk in the main cabin, and an engine tucked away under the cockpit that drives the propeller shaft with V-belts. Nevins built her well, with a double-planked hull and teak decks. She was made shallow for Chesapeake cruising. In contrast to the previous design, which shows a jumper strut and stays for tensioning the jibstay, **Nancy Lloyd** was rigged with running backstays for this purpose.

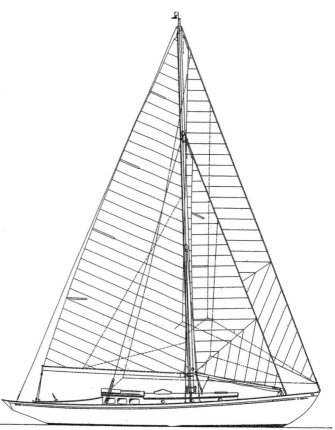

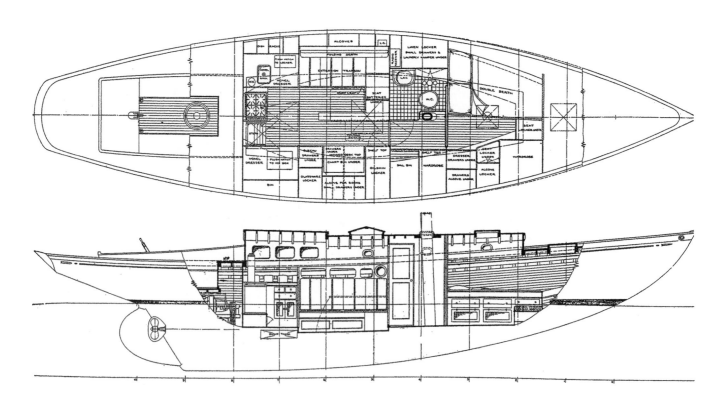

ICE SCOOTER OF 1906
BY H. PERCY ASHLEY

LOA	15'0"
Beam	4'6"
Sail Area	159 sq. ft.
Source	November 1904, pp. 603-6

A boat for all seasons (she'll sail on ice in the winter and in the water during the rest of the year), this scooter is native to Great South Bay on the back side of Long Island, New York. You play the jibsheet to steer, and if you're speeding along on the ice at 25 miles an hour and suddenly hit a hole, it's no problem. With luck, momentum will carry you up again on the ice on the opposite "shore," but with a hoe-ended pike pole (always carried aboard along with oars) you can pull yourself back up on the hard water. Complete plans and specifications are included in the above-referenced source.

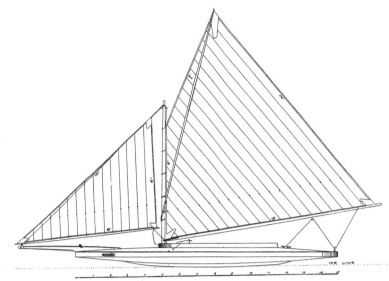

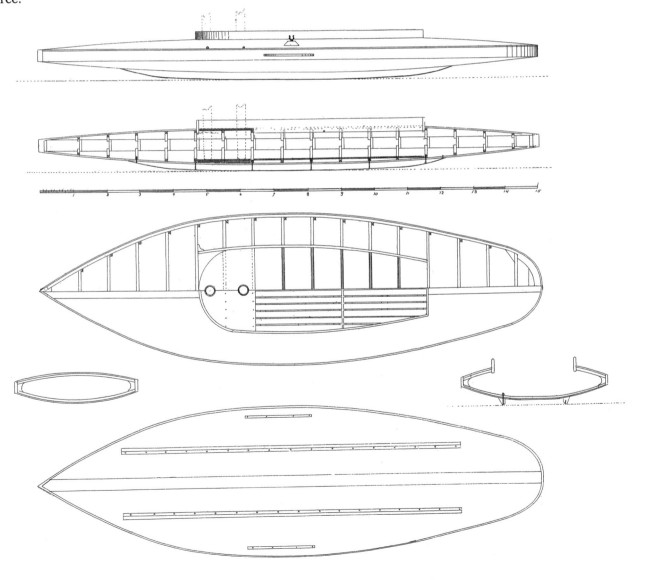

SAILBOATS

YAWLS

CENTERBOARD CRUISING YAWL
OF 1901 BY T. E. FERRIS

LOA	66′ 0″
LWL	45′ 0″
Beam	17′ 0″
Draft	4′ 7″
Source	March 1901, pp. 105-9

Imagine being able to anchor this big yacht in water that's only breast high! Not only is extreme shallow draft unusual in so large a vessel, but there are other items of interest as well. The wooden trunk for the rudderstock, four enclosed staterooms fitted with extra-wide berths, hoisting davits for small boats, and a fo'c's'le for three crew members. This yacht needed a good crew, professionals back then, to tend to her six sails. To tack, for example, there were three headsail sheets, two running backstays, and a mizzen forestay, that had to be let go and taken up on the other side. Not having an engine called for extraordinary seamanship, particularly when getting away from the mooring or picking it up. During such times, a yawl's mizzen, sheeted in, became a blessing and kept her head-to-wind while the remaining sails were being raised or lowered.

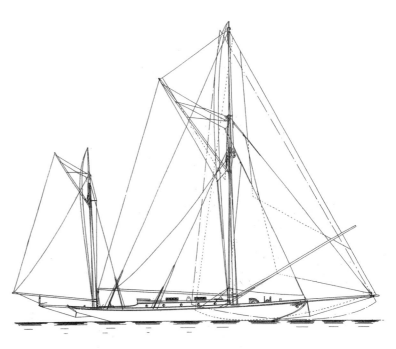

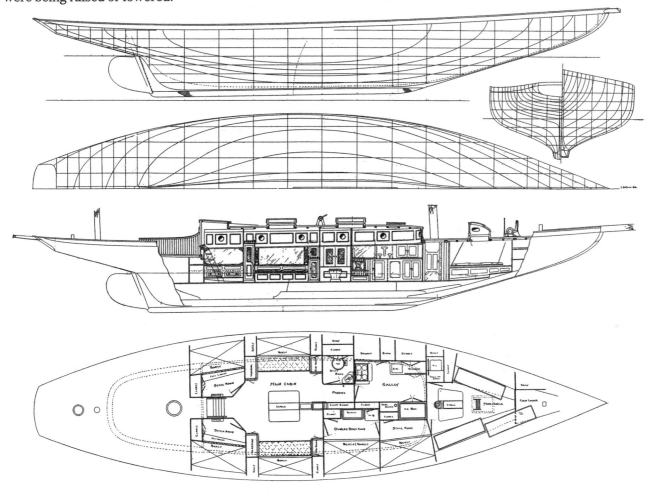

RACING YAWL (OR SLOOP)
OF 1902 BY WILLIAM H. HAND, JR.

LOA 38'4"
LWL 23'6"
Beam 9'6"
Draft 4'6"
Sail Area 794 sq. ft. (yawl rig)
Displ. 10,100 lbs.
Source September 1902, pp. 422-23

Built for racing as a sloop or cruising when rigged
as a yawl, this boat has a fin keel and spade rudder
that make her underbody look decidedly modern.
There's a centerboard, however, that houses within
the fin and leaves the cabin clear of the usual centerboard trunk. She was designed and built to the
rules of the Great Lakes Yacht Racing Union.

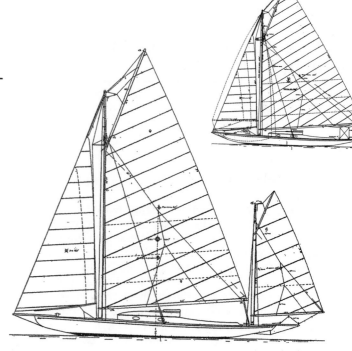

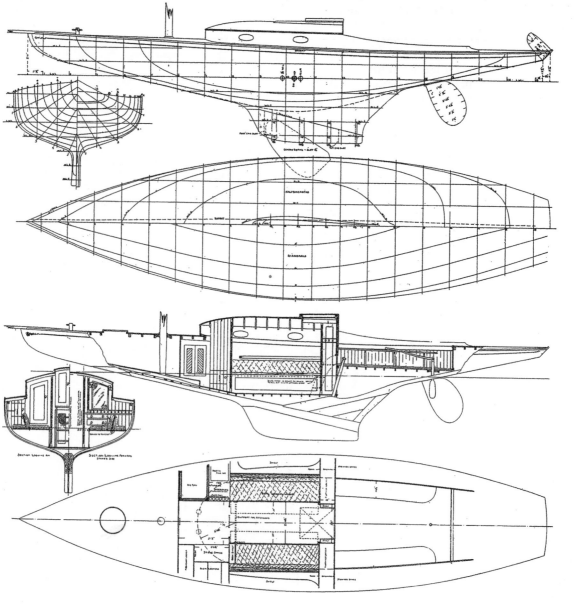

GAFF-RIGGED CRUISING YAWL
QUILL II OF 1905
BY B. B. CROWNINSHIELD

LOA	38'0"
LWL	25'0"
Beam	9'9"
Draft	5'10"
Sail Area	861 sq. ft.
Source	November 1905, pp. 615-17

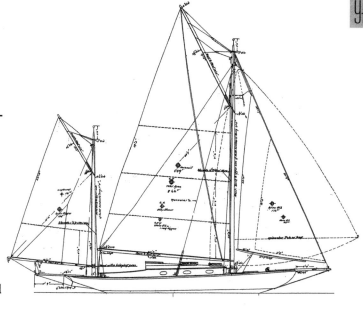

Beautifully built by Hodgdon Bros. of East Boothbay, Maine, **Quill II** still sails and lays claim to being the oldest extant yacht of the many turned out by the Hodgdons. Stepping below, you'd see the same Victorian turned-stanchion rails along the edges of shelves and bureaus, as well as the original leaded-glass locker doors. The rig? The same that shows here. Every fourth frame is double-sawn (molded according to the drawing) to define the hull shape for planking. Later, three intermediate steam-bent frames were slid into each of the initial frame bays and fastened.

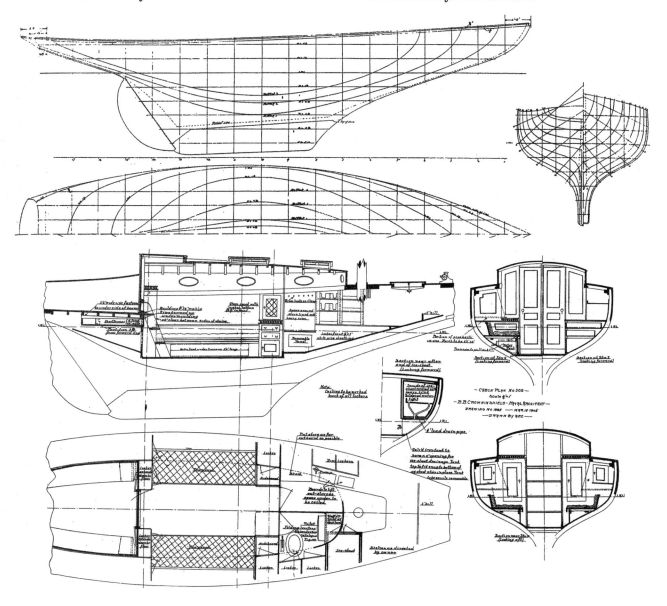

GAFF YAWL OF 1915
BY FREDERICK W. GOELLER, JR.

LOA	45'0"
LWL	38'0"
Beam	12'8"
Draft	6'0"
Sail Area	1,148 sq. ft. (lowers)
Source	June 1915, pp. 294-96

Not quite a motorsailer, yet fitted with a larger-than-usual engine and having a foot or so less draft than you'd expect, this is one fine-looking yacht. Goeller's elegant drafting, of course, could make about any craft look good on paper, but there can be no doubt that the boat herself would be a real beauty. Moderate beam and draft limits the use of the topsails to very light airs, but they sure look good when set. While preparing meals, the paid hand shares the galley with the un-boxed-in engine. He sleeps next to the engine as well, while the owner occupies the fo'c's'le as his private stateroom.

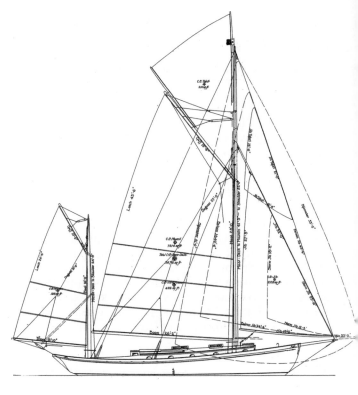

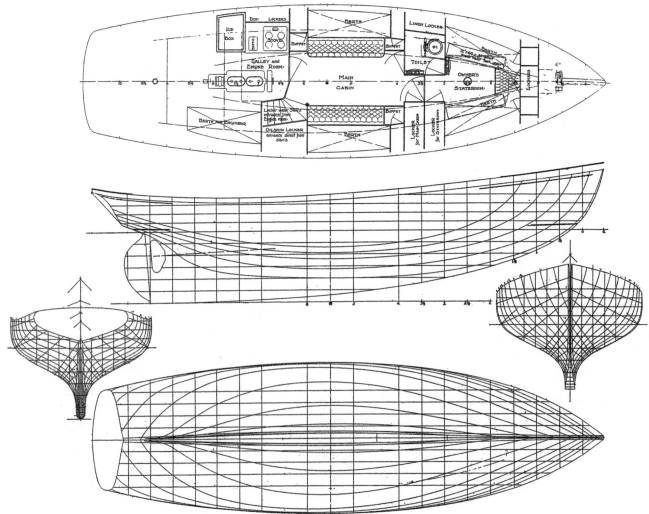

CENTERBOARD CRUISING YAWL
TIPPERARY OF 1917
BY BOWES & MOWER

LOA	60'0"
LWL	44'0"
Beam	14'8"
Draft	6'0"
Sail Area	1,779 sq. ft.
Source	August 1917, pp. 541-42

Tipperary was built by Burger Boat Co. of Manitowoc, Wisconsin, for cruising on the Great Lakes. Besides being lovely to look at, she boasts full headroom under the trunk cabin where you'll find a main cabin with pilot berths for two, a large double stateroom, a full-width galley, an enclosed head, and hanging lockers. The engine is tucked away under the bridge deck, and the centerboard trunk stops short of the cabin sole. More recently, the builder has specialized in large motoryachts with aluminum hulls—a product for which Burger has become widely known.

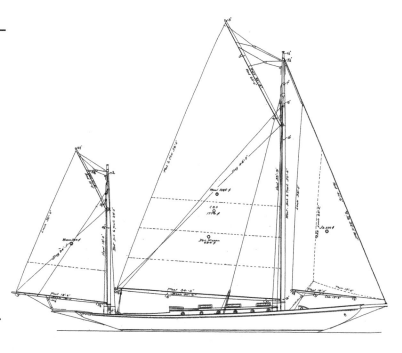

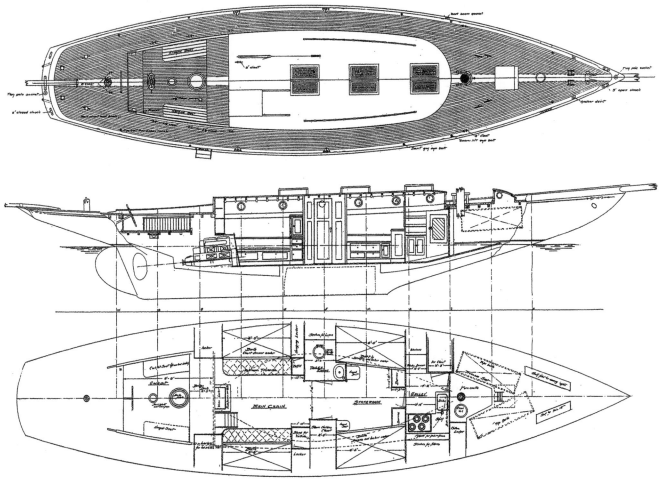

V-BOTTOMED CENTERBOARD YAWL **NAIAD** OF 1904 BY DAY & MOWER

LOA	38′5″
LWL	30′2″
Beam	12′3″
Draft	3′0″
Sail Area	900 sq. ft.
Source	November 1904, pp. 586-91

This is an enlargement of the famous **Sea Bird** in which *The Rudder* editor Thomas Fleming Day crossed the Atlantic a few years earlier. Being half again larger allows for more headroom and decent cruising accommodations for up to six persons. Chine construction with sawn frames make her a relatively easy boat to build; the first boat, from which the name **Naiad** derives, was owner-built for use on the Great Lakes.

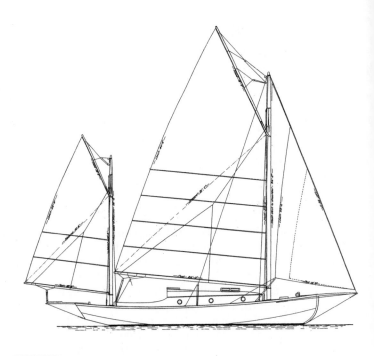

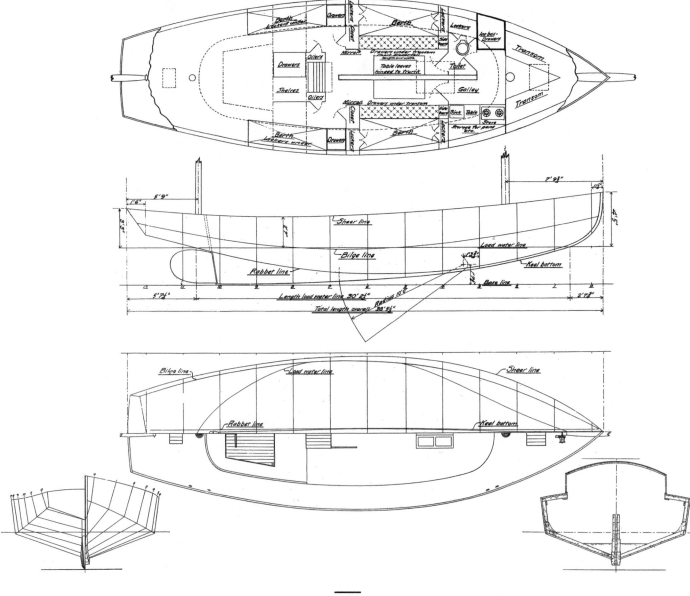

CANOE YAWL OF 1930
BY B. B. CROWNINSHIELD

LOA	32′7″
LWL	23′5″
Beam	5′10″
Draft	4′7″
Sail Area	350 sq. ft.
Displ.	4,923 lbs.
Source	April 1930, p. 49

The simplest boats are sometimes the best. Here's one that's simple as well as striking in appearance—kind of an enlarged Dark Harbor 17-½ footer with a marconi yawl rig. You sit in, not on, this boat because her cockpit is deep and its seats are low. Watertight bulkheads forward and aft form air chambers to keep her afloat in the event of a capsize. In building to this design now, you'd probably want to raise the jibstay nearer to the masthead and eliminate the runners. A permanent backstay from the head of the mainmast to the deck wouldn't be a bad idea, either.

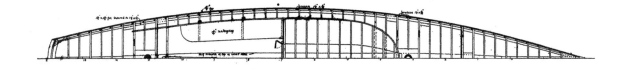

DOUBLE-ENDED POCKET CRUISER
OF 1933 BY FENWICK C. WILLIAMS

LOA	24′0″
LWL	21′6″
Beam	8′8″
Draft	3′9″
Sail Area	318 sq. ft.
Displ.	8,000 lbs.
Source	March 1933, p. 49

Short and fat, yet graceful, this is the opposite extreme from the canoe yawl on the preceding page, although both are singlehanders. Because of her breadth, depth, and full ends, you can make her a comfortable cruiser—as many have done, using a variety of interior arrangements. For more information, take a peek at *WoodenBoat* No. 41 in which **Annie,** a beautifully built yawl of this design, was featured.

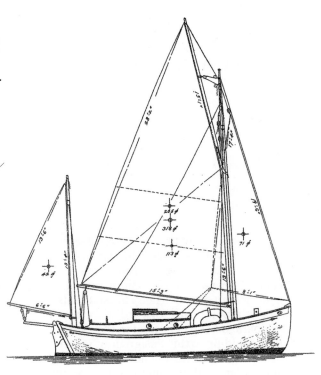

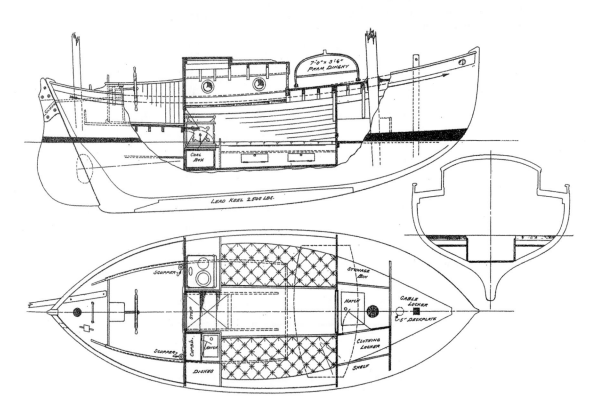

MALABAR JUNIOR OF 1927
BY JOHN G. ALDEN

LOA	30′0″
LWL	23′3″
Beam	9′9″
Draft	5′0″
Sail Area	579 sq. ft.
Source	May 1927, p. 64

Several versions of Malabar Junior emerged from the Alden office during this era, but the earliest ones, of which this is an example, looked best because of their strong sheers, low freeboard, and generally graceful appearance. Here's a handsome cruiser for two (or three in a pinch), with all sheets self-tending so that all one has to do when tacking is spin the wheel.

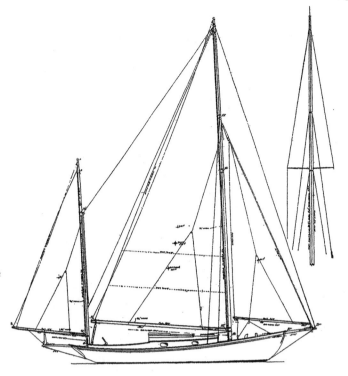

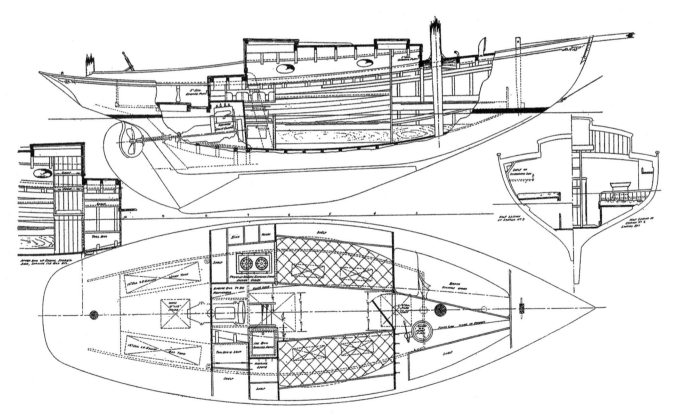

CRUISING YAWLS OF 1936 AND 1939 BY WINTHROP L. WARNER

LOA	34'7"
LWL	27'3"
Beam	11'0"
Draft	5'7"
Source	September 1936, p. 45, and December 1939, p. 38

It's easy to understand why Warner stayed with this hull shape for several iterations after its debut as the designer's own boat in the February 1933 issue of *The Rudder*. That hull is a beauty from any point of view. Note, for example, the hollow forward waterlines and the rolled-in quarters where the sheer meets the transom. The yawls (shown on pages 51 & 52), built as **Meridian, Lenita II,** and **Privateer,** evolved from Warner's own (but never built) cutter and a ketch named **Highlander** whose drawings appeared in *The Rudder* of November 1935. Even in more recent times the design retained its appeal: **Sandpiper,** a ketch, and **Tenacity,** a cutter, were launched in the 1980s.

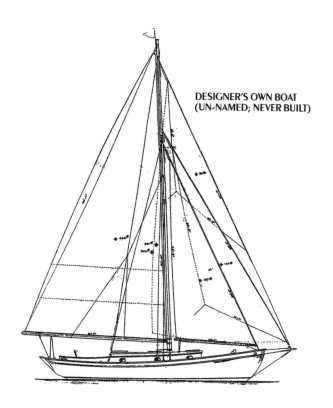

DESIGNER'S OWN BOAT (UN-NAMED; NEVER BUILT)

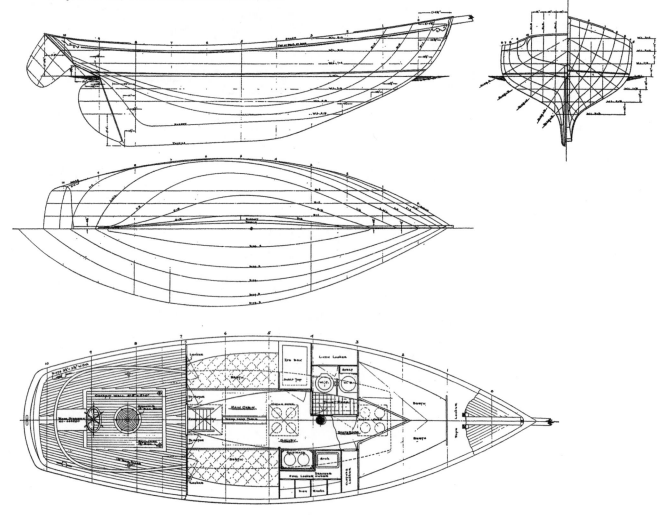

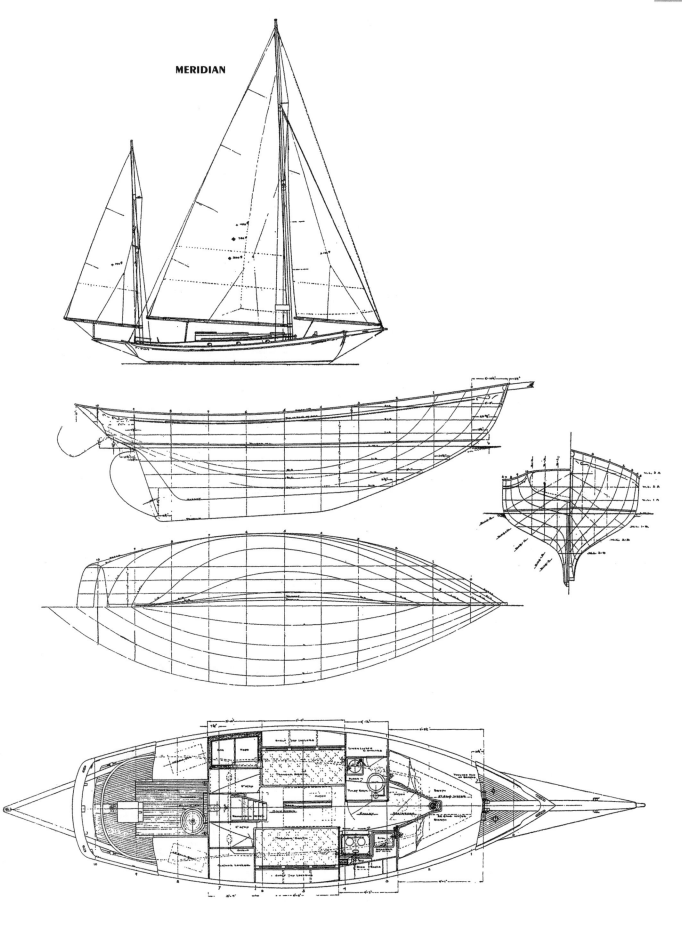

MERIDIAN

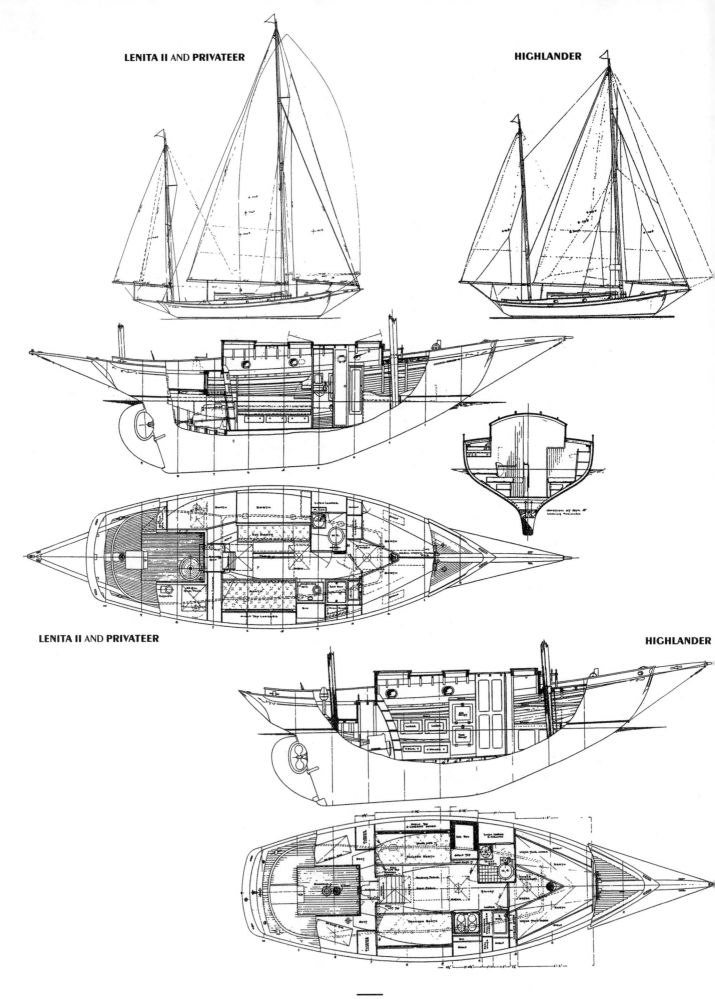

LENITA II AND PRIVATEER

HIGHLANDER

LENITA II AND PRIVATEER

HIGHLANDER

52

GAFF CENTERBOARDER **HERMITA**
OF 1921 BY JOHN G. ALDEN

LOA	47'8"
LWL	37'6"
Beam	13'0"
Draft	5'0"
Sail Area	1,241 sq. ft.
Source	July 1921, pp. 25-26

John Alden could always be depended upon to produce good-looking boats, and **Hermita** is no exception. Above water, except for the rig, she reminds one of Alden's early Malabar schooners that came out about the same time. But this is a centerboarder, able to float in a couple of feet less water. **Hermita** was built by F. F. Pendleton, Wiscasset, Maine.

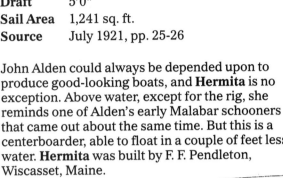

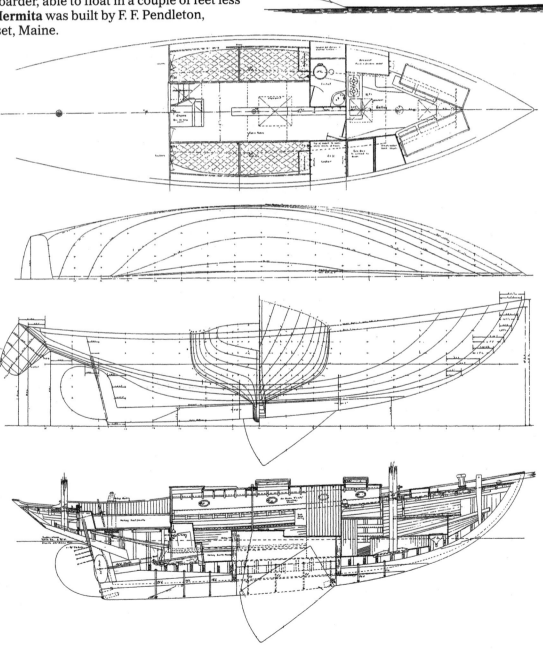

RACER/CRUISER **GOLDEN EYE**
OF 1937 BY PHILIP L. RHODES

LOA	41′0″
LWL	30′0″
Beam	11′0″
Draft	6′0″
Sail Area	900 sq. ft.
Source	August 1937, p. 43

Here's a lovely yawl with a double head rig and an amidships galley, drawn up in typical Rhodes easy-to-read, elegant-to-look-at plans. Boats like this could be either raced or cruised. It's obvious from the drawings that she'd make a wonderful cruiser, but it's harder to predict performance in that manner. Speed under sail for winning races was not a criteria of this design, yet **Golden Eye** proved to do well against competition in her very first race to Gibson Island from New London, Connecticut, when she took Class B honors. **Golden Eye,** built by Minneford Yacht Yard of City Island, New York, still sails on Long Island Sound.

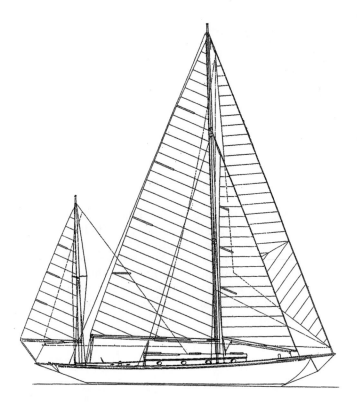

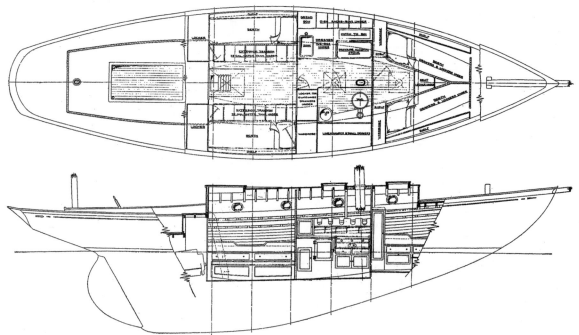

NAVAL ACADEMY YAWLS
OF 1939 BY A. E. LUDERS

LOA	44'0"
LWL	30'0"
Beam	11'0"
Draft	6'0"
Sail Area	900 sq. ft.
Displ.	23,400 lbs.
Source	April 1939, p. 41

With a hull of almost identical dimensions to **Golden Eye** and with exactly the same 900-square-foot sail area, the "Academy Yawls" were fitted with the open sleeping you might expect any training vessel to have. The eight berths left space for a tiny galley and enclosed head and little else, but outwardly, these yawls showed the usual Luders flair for good looks. Intended for use by U.S. Naval Academy cadets, a dozen of these yawls were built by several yards and served well for two decades, despite hard usage, until replaced with fiberglass yawls of similar design.

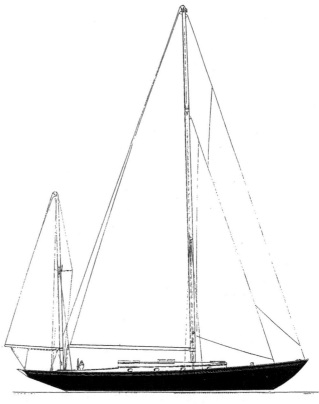

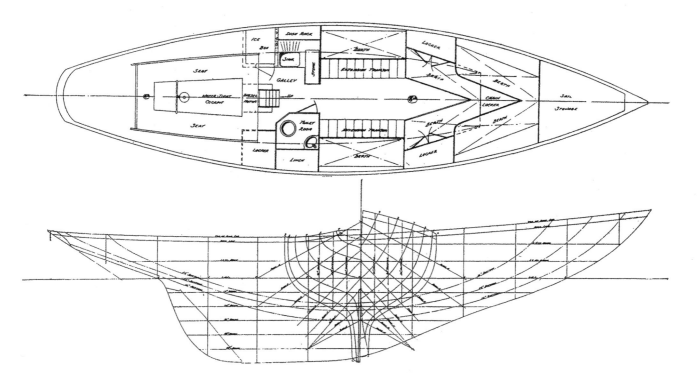

CLIPPER-BOWED RACING YAWL
TIOGA TOO OF 1939
BY JOHN G. ALDEN

LOA	53'6"
LWL	37'9"
Beam	13'0"
Draft	7'5"
Sail Area	1,342 sq. ft.
Source	October 1939, p. 32

Tioga Too slid overboard from Quincy Adams Yacht Yard of Quincy, Massachusetts, three years after her namesake, the 72' ketch now known as **Ticonderoga.** The Noyes family owned both yachts as well as the yard that built them. **Tioga Too,** well sailed by the Noyes boys, won nearly every race she entered. Later named **Burma** and still later **Bellatrix,** she met her end in a boatyard fire of 1964. Her clipper bow, a rare adornment in racing craft, as well as the cutaway forefoot may be carryovers from the family ketch mentioned above, and give this design its distinctive appearance. The off-center companionway, so placed as to not intrude on the owner's cabin, is another feature not often seen.

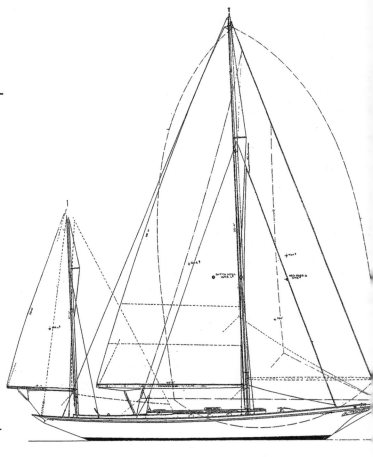

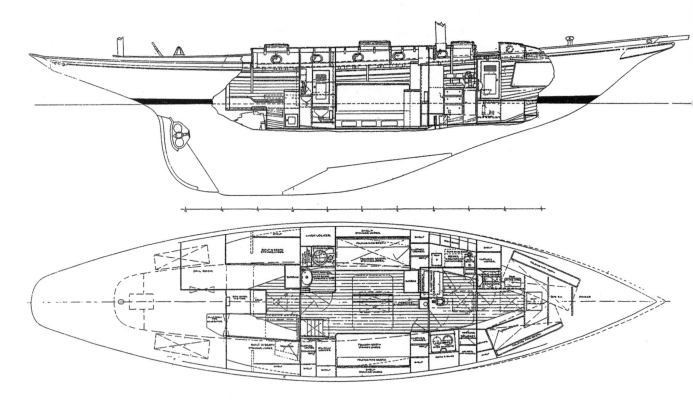

WERDNA OF 1935
BY SPARKMAN & STEPHENS

LOA	40'3"
LWL	30'0"
Beam	10'5"
Draft	6'1"
Sail Area	848 sq. ft.
Source	March 1935, p. 52

Albert Lemos, of Riverside, Rhode Island, built **Werdna,** a nice little boat of the four-berth auxiliary variety. Steering is by wheel, oriented fisherman style. Low bulwarks with a cap are a nice touch and diminish the on-deck presence of the bowsprit and boomkin. Double headsails later gave way to a single, overlapping genoa.

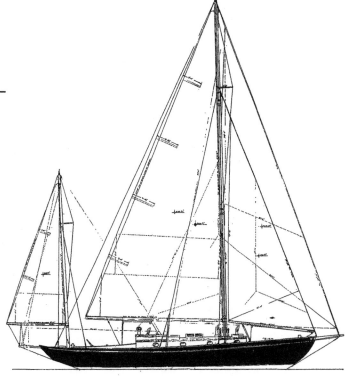

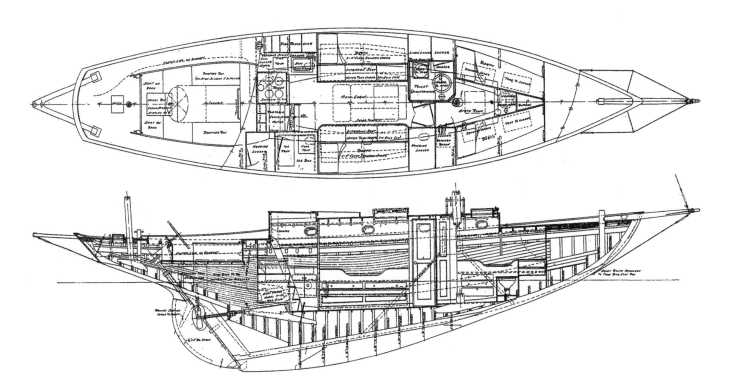

RACING YAWL **AVANTI** OF 1937
BY SPARKMAN & STEPHENS

LOA	55'8"
LWL	40'0"
Beam	12'5"
Draft	7'9"
Sail Area	1,300 sq. ft.
Source	May 1937, p. 48

Sparkman & Stephens yawls evolved as the sailing yacht of choice for many owners during this era, and it's easy to see why. Not only were they extraordinarily graceful, but they had what it took to win races as well. Like **Tioga Too,** already described on page 56, **Avanti** featured an aft cabin for the owner. The main saloon's wrap-around settee to port, and another straight settee opposite to starboard, allowed comfortable seating for a sizeable crowd at mealtime. There's a nav station adjacent to the companionway ladder, with a nearby head—two welcome conveniences for offshore sailing. **Avanti** was beautifully built by Herreshoff Mfg. Co., her hull constructed upside down as was that yard's custom.

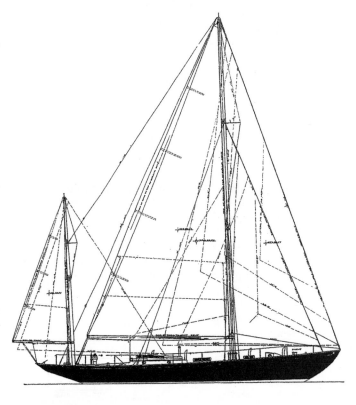

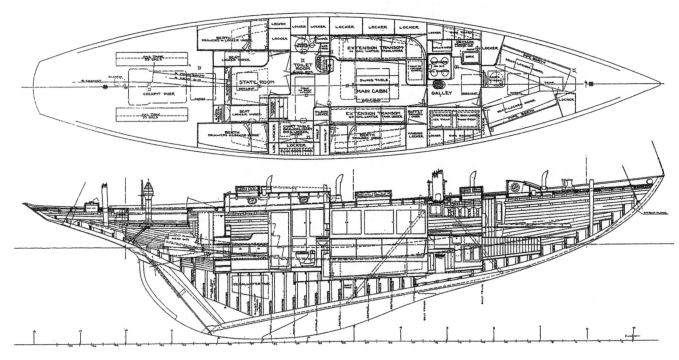

RACING YAWL **EDLU II** OF 1938
BY SPARKMAN & STEPHENS

LOA	68′5″
LWL	48′0″
Beam	14′8″
Draft	9′3″
Sail Area	2,125 sq. ft.
Source	March 1938, pp. 50-51

Measurement rules greatly influence the nature of yachts, and those designed to race under the Cruising Club of America's CCA Rule evolved so they were not only fast, but wholesome and beautiful as well. Yawls were favored in the larger sizes, and one classic CCA yawl after another was launched prior to and following the Second World War. **Edlu II,** built by Nevins of City Island, served owner Rudolph J. Schaefer well in pre-war racing (she came in third after the S&S yawls **Baruna** and **Avanti** in Class A in the 1938 Bermuda Race), and sailed for the decade following the war as Tabor Academy's training vessel. Since 1956, however, this lovely yawl, under the name **Black Watch** and painted white, has been Dr. George Brooks's pride and joy—but as a far-ranging cruiser, not a racer.

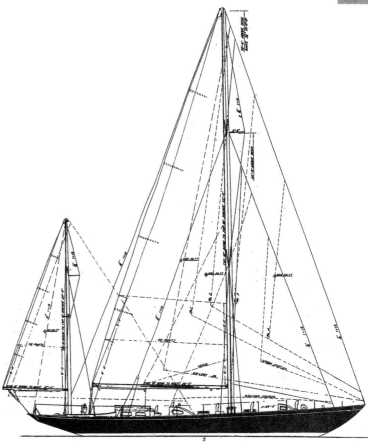

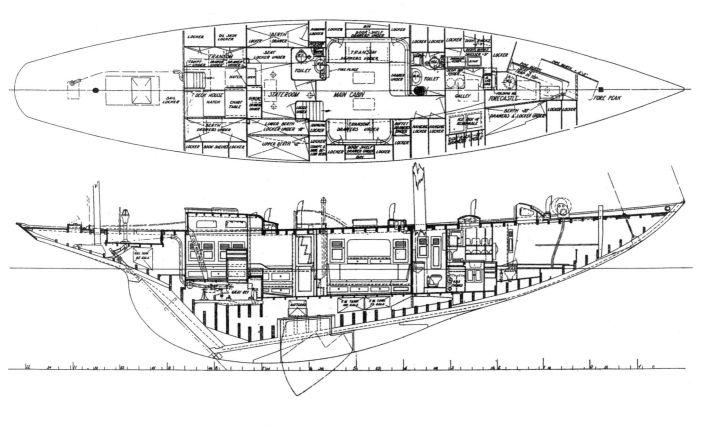

RACING-CRUISING YAWL **TAHUNA** OF 1940 BY PHILIP L. RHODES

LOA	44′3″
LWL	31′0″
Beam	11′3″
Draft	6′6″
Sail Area	989 sq. ft.
Source	September 1940, p. 36

Tahuna's flush foredeck makes for a clear working platform—one that's unobstructed by hatch or trunk cabin. It also gives this lovely yawl her distinctive appearance. Another feature worthy of note is the dual purpose doghouse. It serves as a galley space, or, by placing cushions on the countertops, becomes a seating area with good visibility that's near the cockpit yet sheltered from wind and wave. The engine lives under the doghouse sole, which places it unusually low and allows a horizontal propeller shaft.

In her day, **Tahuna** competed often and with notable success. The Great Lakes were her territory and she took second in the Mackinac Race within two weeks of her launching. Palmer Johnson of Sturgeon Bay, Wisconsin, were the builders.

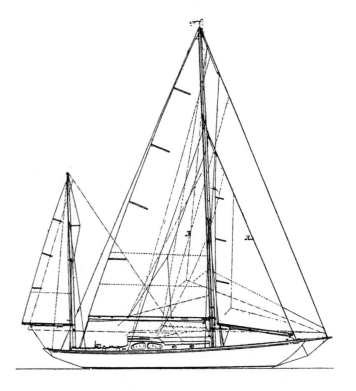

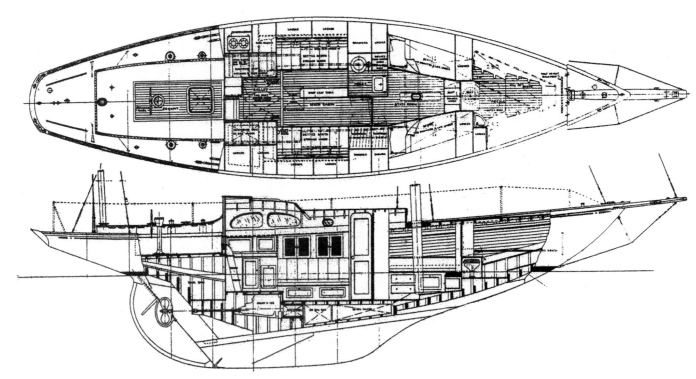

CRUISING/RACING YAWL
ESCAPADE OF 1938
BY PHILIP L. RHODES

LOA	72'6"
LWL	53'0"
Beam	17'0"
Draft	7'6"
Sail Area	2,650 sq. ft.
Source	August 1938, p. 38

While Nevins was building **Edlu II** at City Island, Luders Marine Construction Co. of nearby Stamford, Connecticut, was busy with **Escapade,** both yachts destined to enter the 1938 Bermuda Race. **Escapade** crossed the finish line in third place, but lost out on corrected time to the three Sparkman & Stephens yawls previously mentioned. For headroom, **Escapade** requires a long trunk cabin because of her relatively shallow draft. Her sail-carrying power comes partly from her beam and less from her depth; unlike **Edlu II,** she's a relatively shallow centerboarder. She has the magical Rhodes touch in spite of her generous beam, and looks handsome and powerful under sail. **Escapade,** maintained to perfection, sails now on San Francisco Bay.

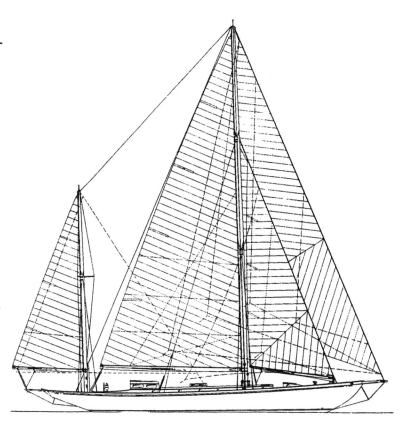

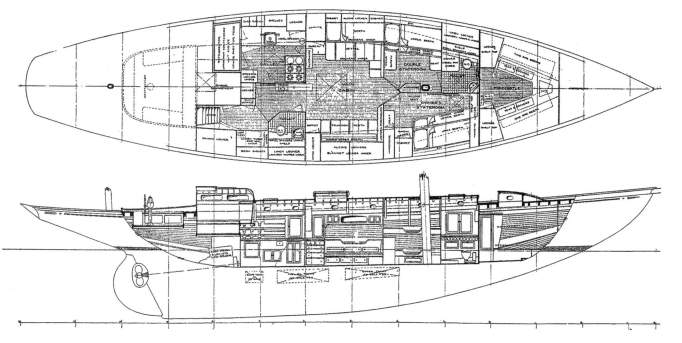

SAILBOATS

KETCHES

SEAGOING CRUISING KETCH
SUNRISE OF 1904
BY WARREN SHEPPARD

LOA	59'3"
LWL	48'3"
Beam	14'4"
Draft	8'0"
Source	January 1904, pp. 18-22

Turn-of-the-century ketches are rare in American yachting, which favored yawls and to some degree schooners. (One disadvantage of a ketch becomes clear if you imagine yourself having to share the cockpit with the low mizzen boom.) But it's hard not to fall in love with this ketch, which looks like she could cross oceans with ease and comfort. She's ruggedly built compared to most yachts of her day with double-sawn frames, a keelson, and deck frame well braced by knees. Designer

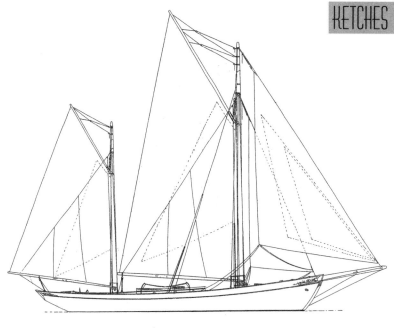

Sheppard was a wonderful artist and supplied *The Rudder* with some lovely art around the time of **Sunrise**'s creation, and occasionally wrote for the magazine as well.

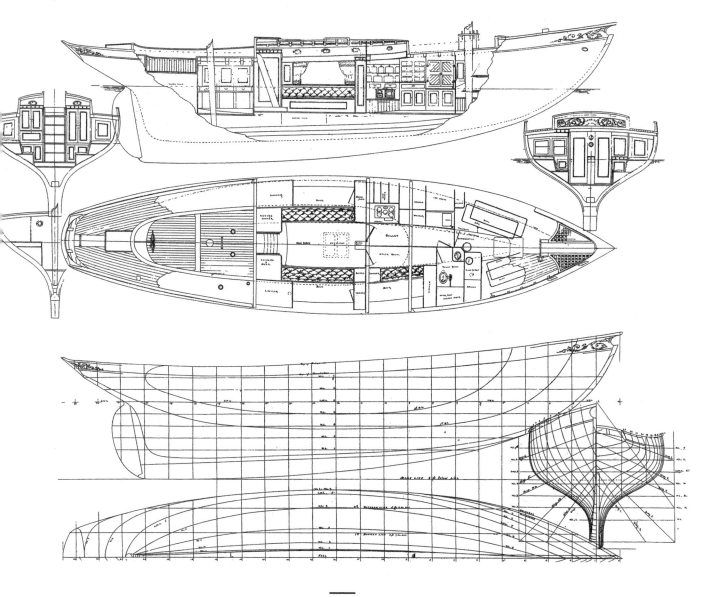

BLOCK ISLAND BOAT **LENA M**, DELINEATED BY MARTIN ERISMANN

LOA	33′7″
LWL	29′5″
Beam	12′4″
Draft	4′0″
Source	April 1912, pp. 266-68

Most traditional working craft got built without benefit of drawings, relying instead on a half model for shape and the builder's experience for construction. But when designer Martin Erismann decided upon a yacht version of a Block Island boat for himself, he carefully measured **Lena M** and drew the accompanying plans. As you can see, accommodations were minimal and the ballast of beach stones was all inside. Seaworthiness is legendary, as Erismann later proved with his own **Roaring Bessie** (not to be confused with Crocker's sloop of the same name shown elsewhere in this book), the adaptation he drew up and had Lawley's build for him in 1911. The main boom on Block Island boats had to be a rugged timber, because the mid-boom sheeting and loose-footed sail combined to produce a significant bending force.

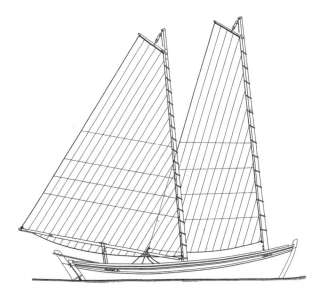

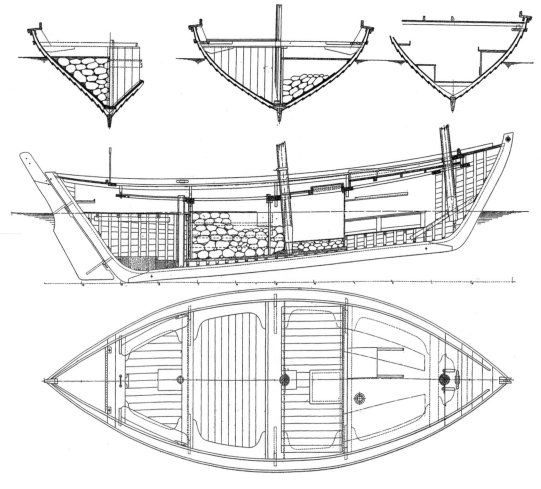

GAFF CRUISING KETCH
TALLAHASSEE OF 1912
BY WILLIAM H. HAND, JR.

LOA	35′0″
LWL	30′3″
Beam	10′0″
Draft	3′6″
Sail Area	560 sq. ft.
Displ.	16,800 lbs.
Source	August 1912, pp. 78-79

Wisely, the designer placed the cockpit of this Lawley-built ketch forward of the mizzen, which provided convenient access to the cabin as well as more headroom under the boom than would have been possible otherwise. The cutaway forefoot, big rudder, dory-type transom, and shallow draft were for running over bars at the mouths of the Florida harbors that were to be part of **Tallahassee**'s cruising grounds. The pair of open-to-the-sea wells in way of the cockpit are to keep fish fresh until eaten or sold. A year later, Hand drew plans for the similar, but deeper and better-known, keel ketch **Fundulus**, which appeared in the March 1913 issue of *The Rudder*.

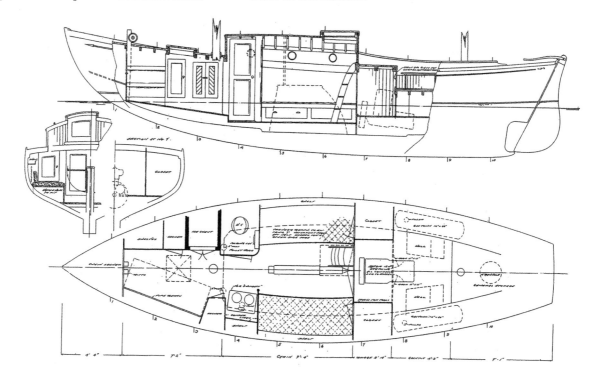

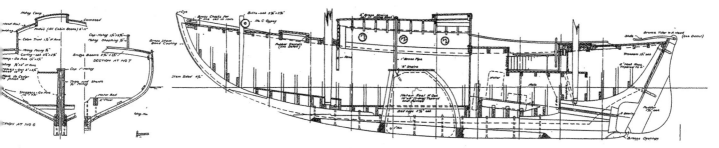

GAFF CRUISING KETCH **SEA DAWN**
OF 1928 BY S. S. CROCKER

LOA	36'0"
LWL	29'0"
Beam	11'0"
Draft	3'6"
Sail Area	672 sq. ft.
Source	January 1928, pp. 52-56, and
	February 1928, pp. 48, 70, 74, 78, 80, 84

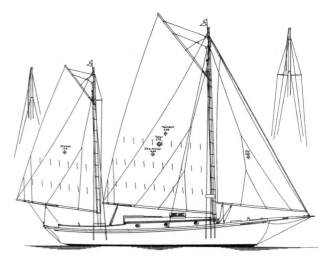

The Rudder featured **Sea Dawn** as a two-part how-to-build article that included complete plans and specifications. She answered the many requests the magazine had received from its readers for a shallow-draft cruiser for four persons; **Sea Dawn** therefore has a centerboard and limited headroom in the cabin. Gaff rigs were becoming rare by the late 1920s when **Sea Dawn** came out, and readers desiring a marconi rig were referred to the designer. Subsequently, *The Rudder* did, however, publish a schooner rig in its June 1929 issue (page 54)—and a staysail schooner at that, without any trace of a gaff!

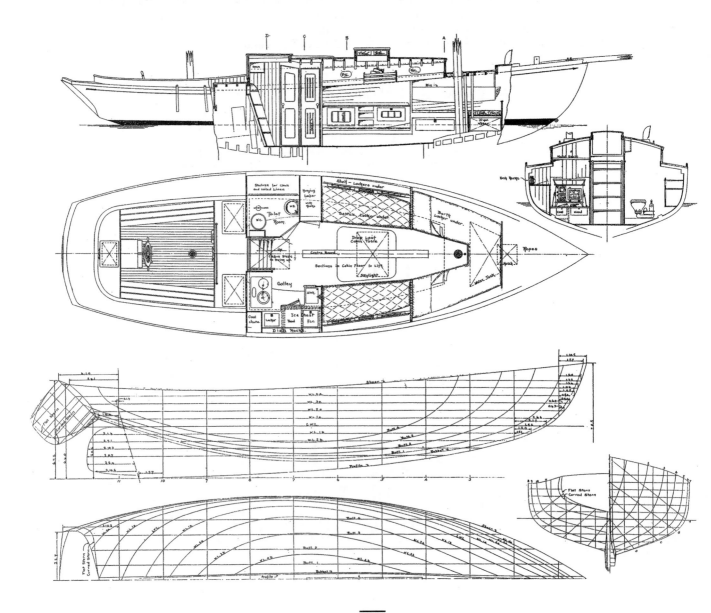

CLIPPER-BOWED KETCH OF 1932
BY MANDELL ROSENBLATT

LOA	38′2″
LWL	30′2″
Beam	12′1″
Draft	5′0″
Sail Area	715 sq. ft.
Source	October 1932, p. 34

In the few yachts this designer created, you can be assured of beauty well beyond the ordinary. (Much of his later career was spent designing steel-hulled military and commercial vessels under the name M. Rosenblatt & Son.) The steam yachts of George Watson served as inspiration for Rosenblatt's lovely bows and sterns, while in this particular design the client requested the rather shallow draft sans centerboard. Not only is this a handsome yacht, but the drawings are especially attractive as well. Although a galley aft by the companionway is convenient, a galley located forward as shown that can be completely shut off from the main cabin also has its advantages. By hinging the backs of the settees so they'll swing up to form upper berths, the designer has set up the main cabin to sleep four persons.

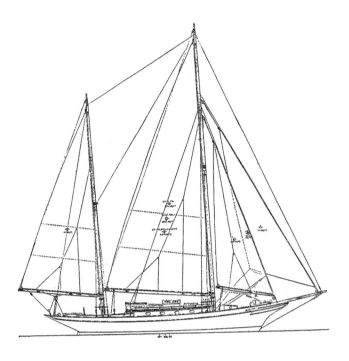

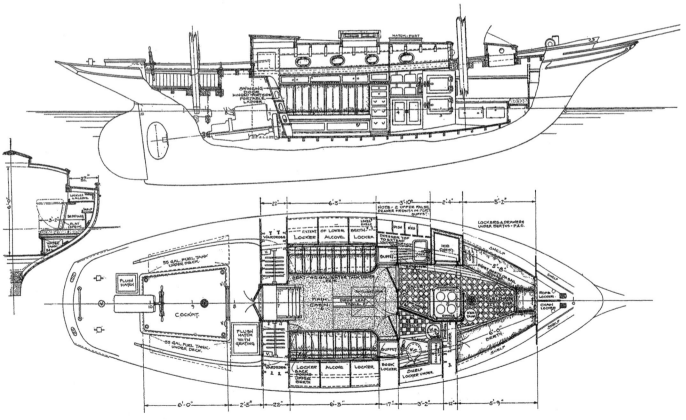

DOUBLE-ENDED KETCH
DOG STAR OF 1934
BY PHILIP L. RHODES

LOA	30'8"
LWL	27'1"
Beam	10'2"
Draft	5'0"
Sail Area	545 sq. ft.
Source	March 1934, p. 44

Dog Star is a development of an earlier Rhodes double-ended ketch named **Tidal Wave** that received a good deal of publicity because of her better-than-expected speed under sail. Both boats are fat double-enders, at least at first glance, but further study reveals a narrower waterline beam and decent sailing lines as well as a tall and reasonably efficient rig. If you're after a seakindly boat that's comfortable in about any weather, and want to keep to a short overall length, this design bears serious consideration. M. M. Davis & Sons of Solomons, Maryland, built **Dog Star**.

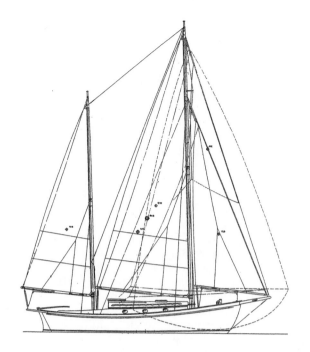

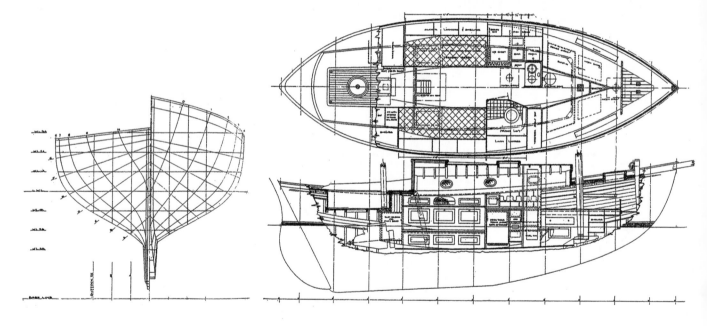

BUGEYE YACHT **BEN GUNN**
OF 1938 BY S.S.CROCKER

LOA	37′ 7″
LWL	32′8″
Beam	10′6″
Draft	3′0″
Sail Area	637 sq. ft.
Source	February 1938, p. 42

Designed along the lines of a Chesapeake Bay bugeye and given a centerboard to keep the draft shallow for Florida cruising, **Ben Gunn** also features a separate aft cabin where two can sleep (and from which engine access is gained). The low and narrow doghouse allows one to stand upright while preparing meals, although drop seats hinged from the centerboard trunk make inviting seating for cooking and eating. Bugeyes have limited sail-carrying ability because of their shallow draft, so the rig has to be kept small. There are many sail combinations possible with a ketch, and one of the handiest tricks is simply to drop the mainsail when it breezes up. Shrouds run to the tops of the masts, and the foremast is rigged with ratlines so one can climb to the top and scout the transparent, southern waters for navigable depth. Simms Bros. of Dorchester, Massachusetts, built **Ben Gunn**.

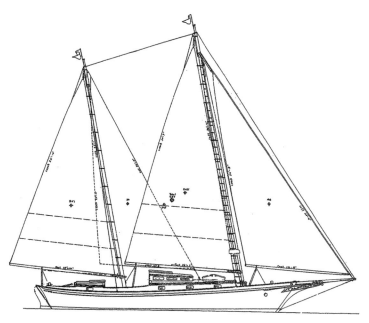

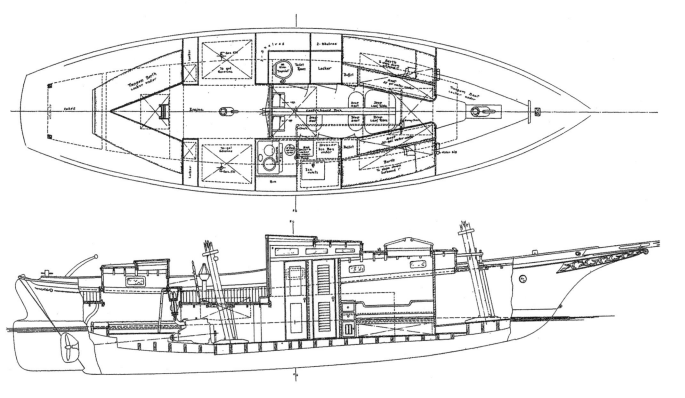

GAFF CRUISING KETCH
PROSPECTOR OF 1940
BY CONCORDIA CO.

LOA	42'9"
LWL	38'6"
Beam	12'6"
Draft	6'0"
Sail Area	923 sq. ft.
Displ.	37,800 lbs.
Source	May 1942, pp. 36-37

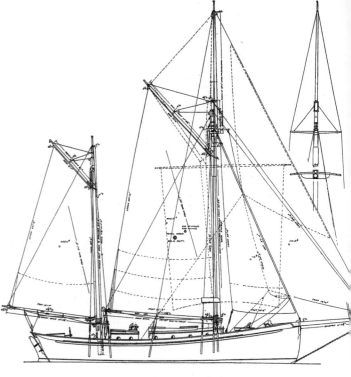

When virtually complete, the first yacht built to this design perished in a fire. The second, built in Florida, was altered a bit from what's shown here in that she had a marconi mizzen stepped further aft, a small doghouse, and some interior layout changes. Wilder B. Harris actually drew these plans while he worked for Concordia and produced an exceptionally salty design, but the experienced thinking of (and massive correspondence between) Waldo Howland and owner Jack Harper played a vital role as well. **Prospector** was designed for offshore cruising and living aboard;

in fact, under a subsequent owner, she sailed around the world. **Prospector**'s creation has been chronicled in detail by Waldo Howland in his book *A Life in Boats: The Early Years*.

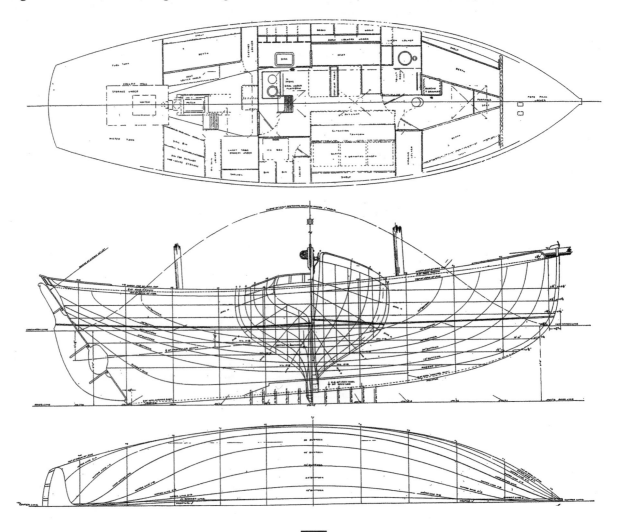

H-28 CRUISING KETCH OF 1943 BY L. FRANCIS HERRESHOFF

LOA	28'0"
LWL	23'2"
Beam	8'9"
Draft	3'6"
Displ.	9,017 lbs.
Source	January 1943, pp. 50-53; February 1943, pp. 20-22; March 1943, pp. 38-41; April 1943, pp. 36-39, 58-60; May 1943, pp. 14-15; June 1943, pp. 38-39; August 1943, pp. 25-28, 52; November 1943, pp. 16-17; December 1943, p. 33; January 1944, pp. 56-57

One of Boris Lauer-Leonardi's first moves when he took over as *The Rudder*'s editor in 1942 was to commission this design from L. Francis Herreshoff. It became a wartime dreamboat, presented in a series of ten how-to-build articles with evocative and carefully detailed drawings, run large. More LFH designs followed, but of all of them, this relatively easy-to-build ketch claimed first place as most popular. "The editor," as L. Francis called Boris in print, had one built for himself at the war's end, and an H-28 owners club came into being soon after this design was published. H-28s are a little tender because of shallow draft and slack bilges, and aren't very speedy, but on paper as well as in real life they look so "right" it's easy to understand why many were built. A number of modifications were made to provide full headroom, always at some sacrifice in looks. The basic design was lengthened as well, independently, and offered as a stock boat called the Bermuda 30.

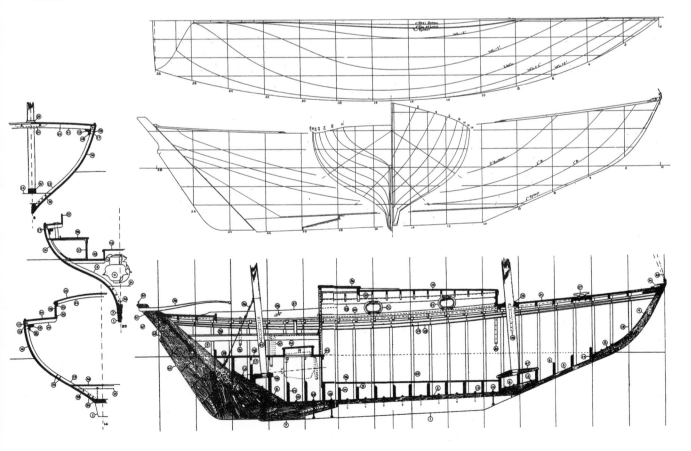

SAILBOATS

SCHOONERS

SHALLOW-DRAFT KEEL SCHOONER **GREY GULL II** OF 1933 BY S.S. CROCKER

LOA	36′2″
LWL	32′2″
Beam	11′1″
Draft	4′6″
Sail Area	847 sq. ft.
Source	September 1933, p. 34

A hollow bow, a wineglass stern, a springy sheer, and the romance of a schooner rig. What more could one ask for? **Grey Gull** will sleep six instead of the customary four found in most boats of this size, and there's good seating in the forwardmost of her two cabins. The only penalty for these features is a galley and an enclosed head that are a little smaller than usual. Another trade-off worthy of mention is her shallow draft, which comes at a sacrifice in the ability to carry full sail to windward in a blow. A later schooner built to this design named **Maccoboy** (now **Nylla**) was made deeper.

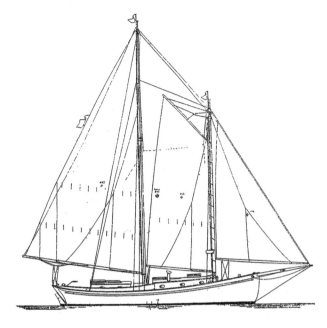

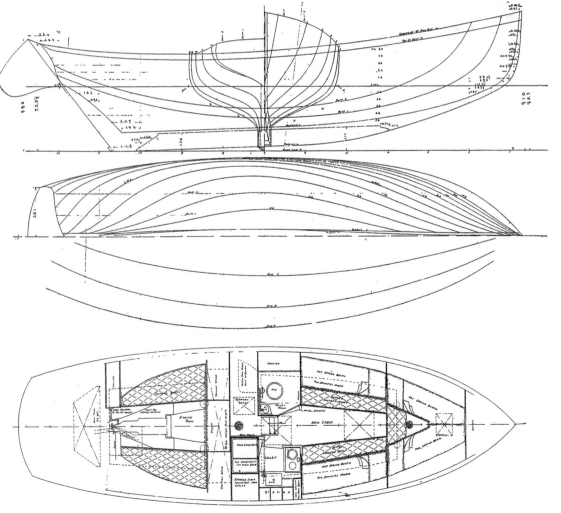

SHORT-ENDED GAFF SCHOONER
VOYAGER OF 1923
BY WILLIAM H. HAND, JR.

LOA	35′0″
LWL	31′6″
Beam	11′3″
Draft	6′0″
Sail Area	704 sq. ft.
Source	March 1923, pp. 51-53 and April 1923, pp. 22-24

Bill Hand always favored high bows, and the way he combined them with the rest of a design for an overall shippy and harmonious look marked him as one of our greatest designers ever. Hand drew this boat especially for *The Rudder*, which featured her as a two-part how-to-build article with complete plans, a table of offsets, and detailed specifications that an experienced builder could work from. In this case, you'll not find the step-by-step instructions for a first-time worker.

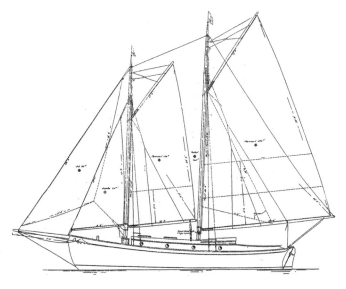

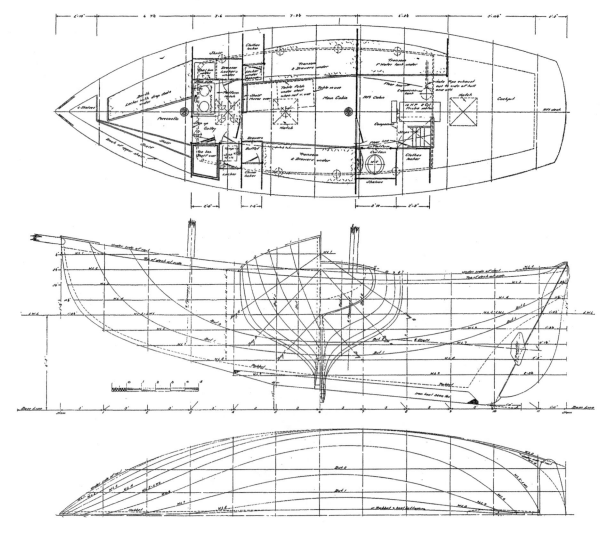

COASTING SCHOONER **COASTER**
OF 1932 BY MURRAY G. PETERSON

LOA	36'4"
LWL	29'8"
Beam	11'2"
Draft	5'9"
Sail Area	796 sq. ft.
Source	August 1932, p. 38

This is the first of three schooner-yachts that
Peterson designed and had built for his own use—
all carrying the name **Coaster.** Peterson conceived
them as small and fancy editions of the once ubiquitous commercial vessels that carried cargo up
and down the New England coast. Although
Murray Peterson designed a wide range of yachts,
he is remembered mostly for his finely executed
schooners, like this one, built by Goudy & Stevens
of East Boothbay, Maine, that fairly dripped with
traditional detail.

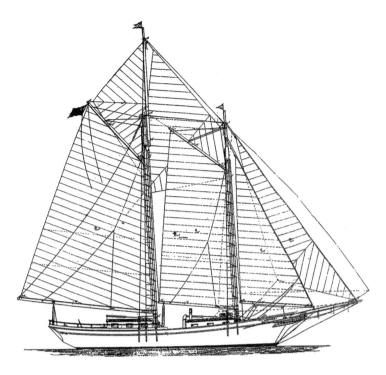

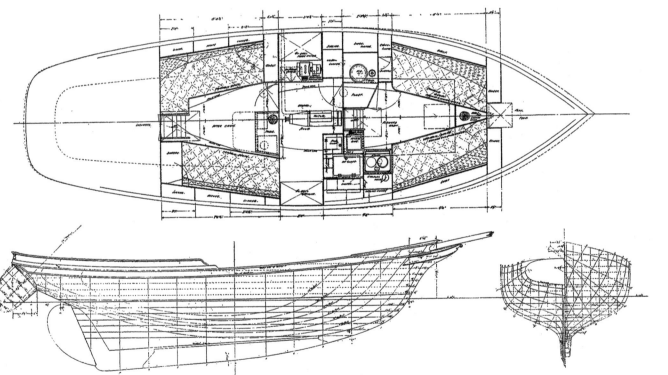

GAFF SCHOONER **MALABAR III**
OF 1923 BY JOHN G. ALDEN

LOA	41′6″
LWL	32′0″
Beam	11′3″
Draft	6′2″
Sail Area	945 sq. ft.
Source	January 1923, p. 41

Fishing schooners rather than coasting schooners inspired John Alden, and, like Peterson, he designed and commissioned several for himself. He named all his personal yachts **Malabar**. This is typical of his first three; his later **Malabar**s gradually grew in size. Schooners like these can be plainly finished, without any varnish at all, and still look appropriate. So treated, maintenance can be cut way down.

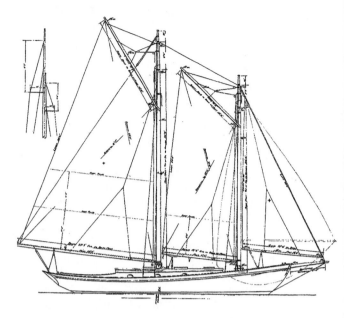

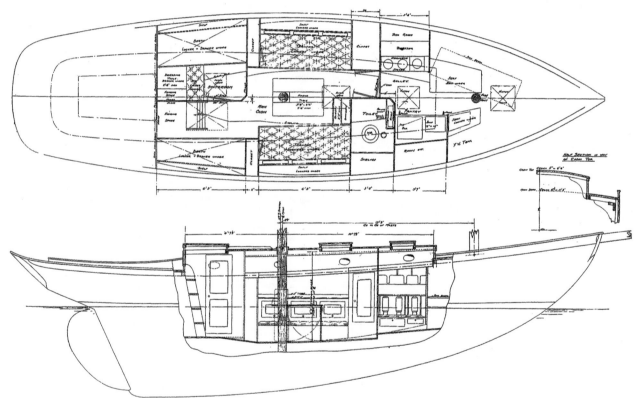

KNOCKABOUT SCHOONER
EASTWARD OF 1928
BY ELDREDGE-McINNIS

LOA	45'0"
LWL	38'0"
Beam	11'6"
Draft	6'5"
Sail Area	918 sq. ft.
Source	November 1928, pp. 45-46

Harvey Gamage of South Bristol, Maine, built the original **Eastward,** and great fanfare accompanied her creation. Others were subsequently built to this design, with at least one of them rigged as a cutter and sailing today as **Prowess.** To eliminate the need for a bowsprit, Walter McInnis, who actually drew the plans, gave her a generous forward overhang, and with it the short stern to produce a most distinctive profile. Below, the big galley and a centerline, enclosed head are worth noting.

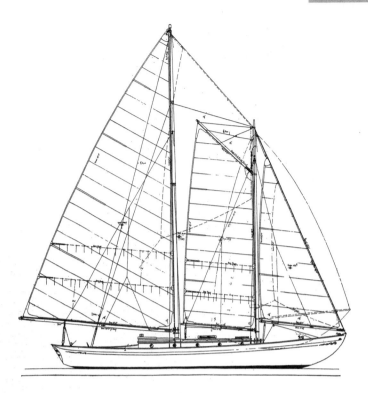

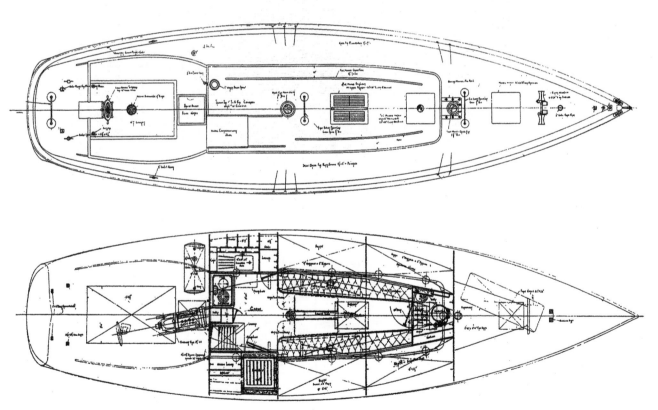

FISHERMAN-TYPE SCHOONER
BLACK HAWK OF 1922
BY WILLIAM H. HAND, JR.

LOA	63′3″
LWL	48′0″
Beam	16′0″
Draft	8′4″
Sail Area	1,866 sq. ft.
Source	June 1922, p. 28

Designers who own and sail the yachts built from the designs they specialize in continue to excel. Alden and Hand clearly dominated the schooner world during the 1920s with their inspired creations. Hand schooners, like his own **Black Hawk** shown here, tended toward high bows, deep draft aft, and small foresails. Unlike most designers, his depictions faced left instead of right. True to her heritage, **Black Hawk** spent her final years as a commercial fisherman.

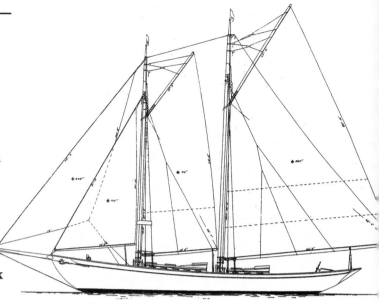

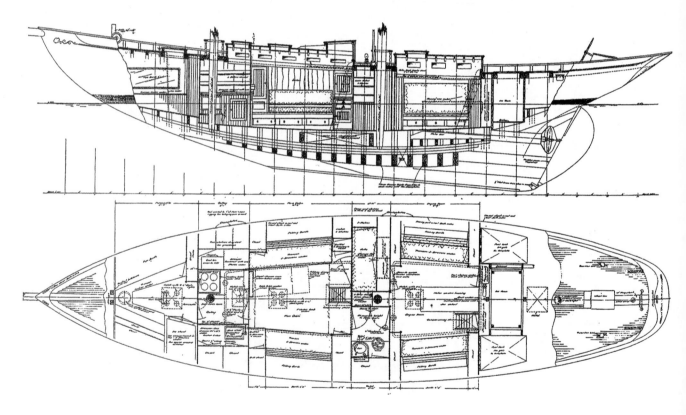

RACING SCHOONER OF 1912 BY B.B. CROWNINSHIELD

LOA	40'11"
LWL	30'0"
Beam	7'11"
Draft	5'11"
Sail Area	770 sq. ft.
Source	February 1912, pp. 96-97

Designed for speed and easy handling—and as a one-design class for racing—this is a slippery but simple little yacht. Boys of the yachtsman-to-be variety could learn how to sail and race as well as gain experience with topsails and staysails in this relatively inexpensive craft. Several were built by Rice Brothers of East Boothbay, Maine, for use on Long Island Sound. If one kept to the original simplicity, a schooner built to this design would be a mighty fine young person's cruiser today despite her scant headroom.

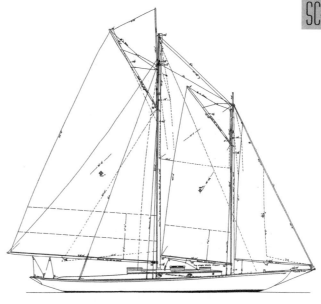

The plans for a similar, but slightly larger schooner named **Heron** were published a month earlier in the January issue of *The Rudder* (pages 44-45). **Heron** is less of a racer and more of a cruiser; her dimensions are LOA 45'6", LWL 33'0", beam 9'2", and draft 6'3".

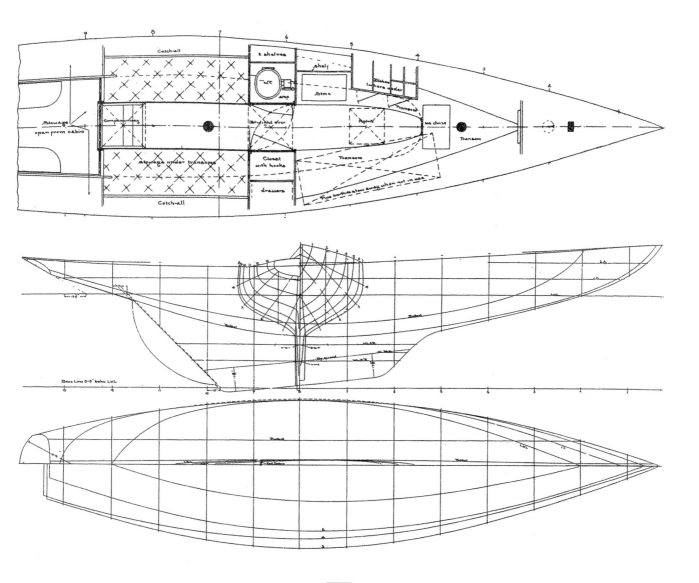

CRUISING SCHOONER OF 1901
BY B.B. CROWNINSHIELD

LOA	56'3"
LWL	35'0"
Beam	13'4"
Draft	7'7"
Source	March 1901, pp. 99-102

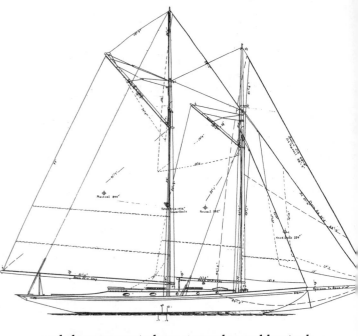

For some more comfortable cruising than the schooner discussed on the previous page can offer, you might try this one—called "a small cruising schooner" by *The Rudder*. She's a full-keeled model but without excessive draft, and for sport and speed during light weather can fly a main topsail, a jib topsail, and a fisherman staysail. Her foresail is double-sheeted since it overlaps the mainmast and must be let go and trimmed with each new tack. Her hull, deck, and even her cabintop are diagonally strapped for strength; she has double-sawn frames except at the bow and stern, and she appears to have a wooden rudderstock. Below deck, her main cabin—which surrounds the butt of the mainmast— would be unusually snug and cozy.

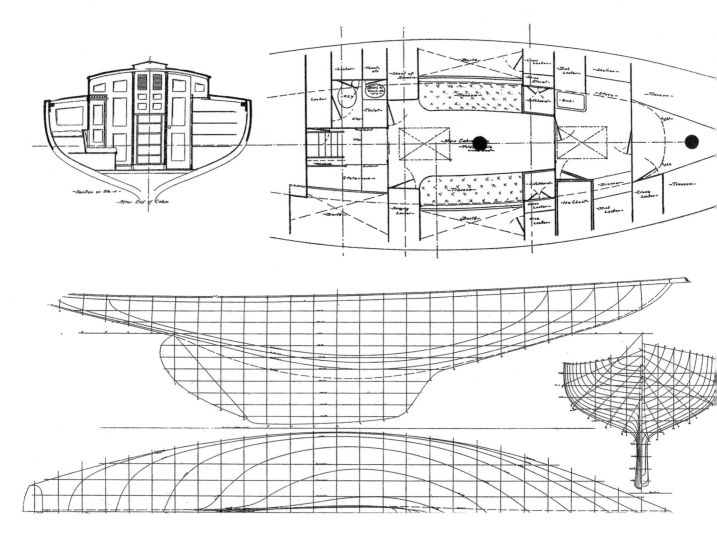

CRUISING SCHOONER **BONITA**
OF 1901 BY LEIGH H. COOLIDGE

LOA	66′6″
LWL	44′0″
Beam	15′1″
Draft	8′8″
Displ.	56,000 lbs.
Sail Area	2,135 sq. ft. (lowers only)
Source	May 1901, pp. 238-39

There's nothing quite like a jackyard topsail to set
a boat apart. It's purely a light-weather sail, of
course, but must have been worth the trouble in
these early yachts without auxiliary power. One
wonders why these wonderful yachts disap-
peared after only a few years' use. Despite her
century-old design, a wholesome craft like
this, with her moderate draft and sweet hull
shape, would still work for cruising today—
although you'd probably want to give her a more
easily handled rig, without that jackyard topsail.

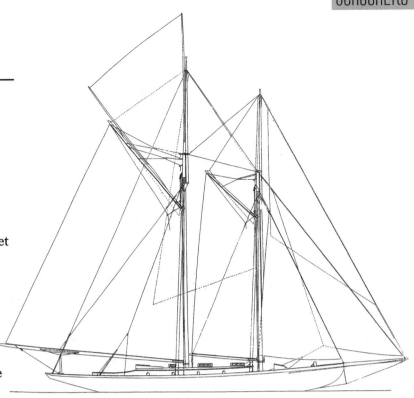

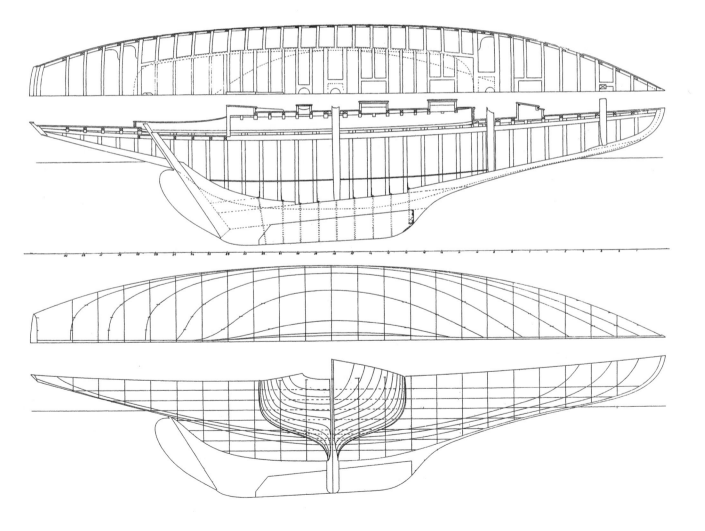

GAFF CRUISING SCHOONER
WANDERER IX OF 1921
BY CHARLES D. MOWER

LOA	65′0″
LWL	44′3″
Beam	15′4″
Draft	8′0″
Sail Area	1,822 sq. ft.
Source	January 1922, pp. 24-25

An after stateroom given over to the owner shows up in sizable sailing yachts like this because of the privacy it affords. And in these large yachts, the galley almost always falls adjacent to the crews' quarters, because there'll be a professional cook. If any overnight guests come aboard, they'll sleep in the main cabin, which, by swinging up the backs of the settees to form uppers, can sleep four. (The settees themselves form the lowers.) By day, the main cabin is where meals are taken; its ambiance also encourages good conversation. A. O. Miller of Riverside, Rhode Island, built this handsome schooner.

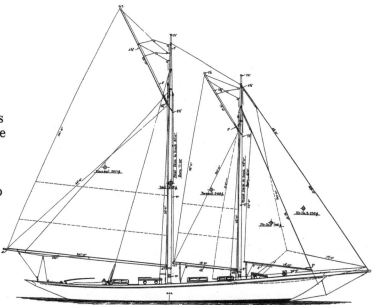

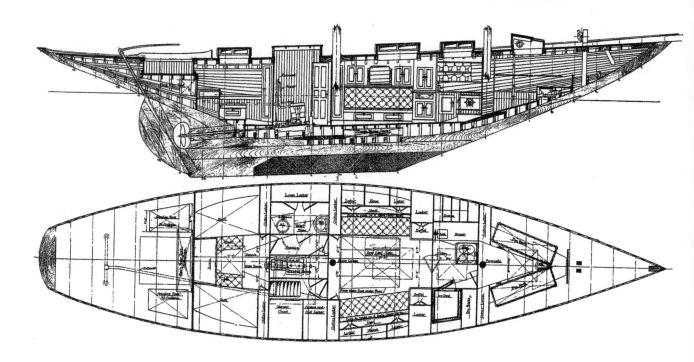

CRUISING SCHOONER **HATHOR II**
OF 1930 BY JOHN G. ALDEN

LOA	84′0″
LWL	64′0″
Beam	18′0″
Draft	10′2″
Sail Area	3,024 sq. ft.
Source	June 1930, p. 53

The professional captain enjoyed his own private stateroom in this big schooner, and there's a double bed in the owner's stateroom way aft. There's even a bathtub! *The Rudder*'s writeup called her a "typical Alden schooner," signifying that by the 1930s schooners from this design office were easily recognized. By then, Alden had had a decade of experience in yachts of this type, but it seems that any type of craft drawn by Alden and his staff looked uncommonly handsome. Likewise, Hodgdon Bros. of East Boothbay, Maine, consistently turned out well built yachts, so **Hathor II** must have been a beautiful sight on launching day.

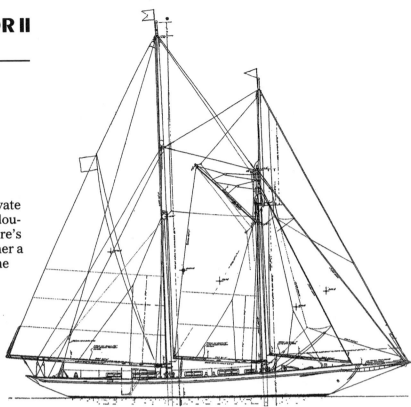

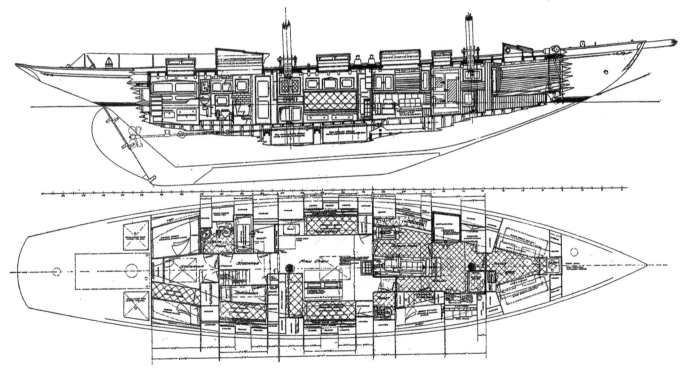

SEAGOING SCHOONER **PILGRIM**
OF 1934 BY JOHN G. ALDEN

LOA	85′0″
LWL	70′0″
Beam	20′8″
Draft	10′8″
Sail Area	2,882 sq. ft. (lowers only)
Source	March 1934, p. 50

Created for the express purpose of sailing around the world, **Pilgrim** accomplished what she set out to do. She's fitted with a yard and squaresails on the foremast for tradewind sailing, while inspiration for the overall design comes partly from fishing schooners and partly from coasting schooners. **Pilgrim** was built by the Reed-Cook Construction Co. of Boothbay Harbor, Maine. More about this husky vessel's circumnavigation can be found in the new book *The Schooner* **Pilgrim**'s *Progress*, written by owner Donald Starr. **Pilgrim**, under the name **Tiki**, subsequently starred in the television series *Adventures in Paradise*.

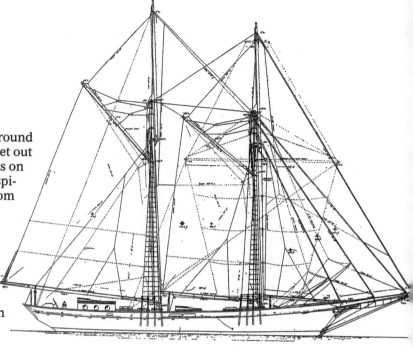

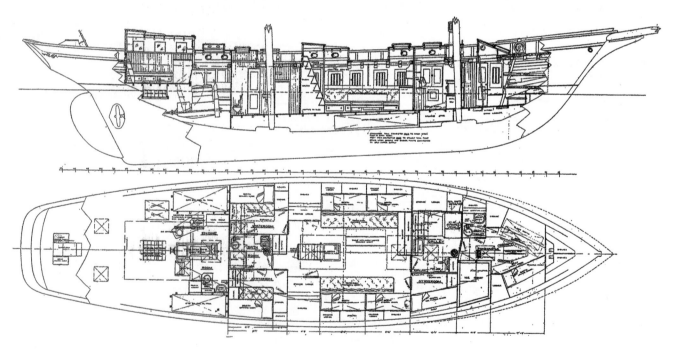

SHOAL-DRAFT CRUISING SCHOONER OF 1899 BY B.B. CROWNINSHIELD

LOA	94'4"
LWL	70'0"
Beam	23'10"
Draft	3'0"
Sail Area	3,989 sq. ft.
Source	September 1899, pp. 339-42

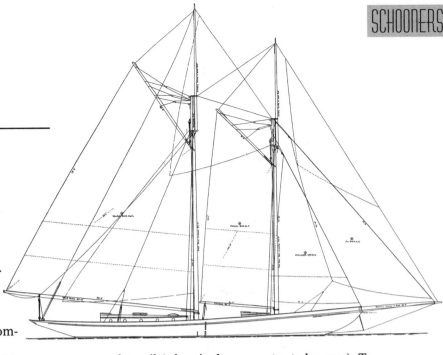

Being able to sail, or at least float, in water a yard deep with a vessel this big seems like a tall order. But it's an interesting idea, and it's also interesting to see how designer Crowninshield carried out this commission. This schooner was to be used at times as a base lodge while the owner and his guests went duck hunting, so she carried a power launch, a cutter, and a dinghy, all of which could be hoisted on davits. Her huge centerboard, when raised, projected above the deck and when lowered kept her from making excessive leeway under sail (when in deeper water to be sure). To aid in steering, a daggerboard was fitted just ahead of the rudder. Heavy construction and considerable inside lead ballast helped, along with a generous beam, to give this schooner the stability needed to carry a rig of conventional proportions.

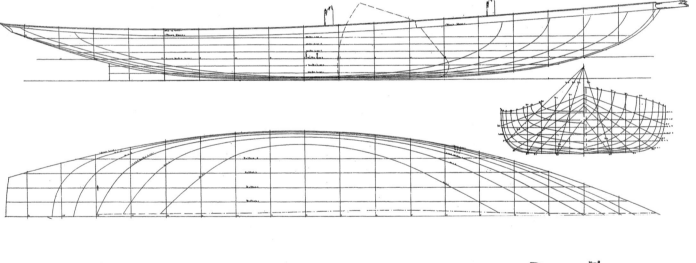

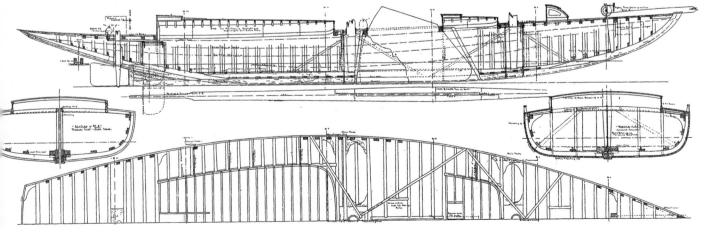

GAFF SCHOONER YACHT **VALMORE** OF 1904 BY FRED D. LAWLEY

LOA 81′3″
LWL 51′3″
Beam 16′0″
Sail Area 3,120 sq. ft. (lowers only)
Source March 1904, pp. 130-31

Owner to starboard (the favored side in any vessel) and toilet room to port; an after stateroom for guests and a sleeping cabin for the professional captain; crew berthing in the fo'c's'le adjacent to the galley—all just the way a proper yacht of this size should be. Lawley built as well as Lawley designed meant wonderful workmanship to go with this fine design. Judging from what detail shows up on the drawing of the yacht's inboard profile, carvings and raised panels abounded. Inside or out, **Valmore** was a mighty handsome creation.

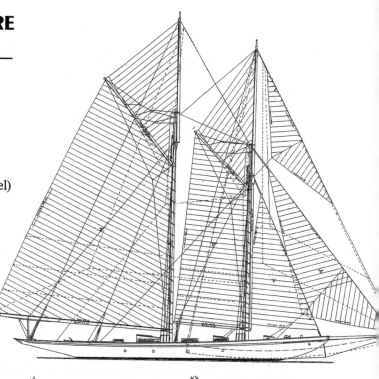

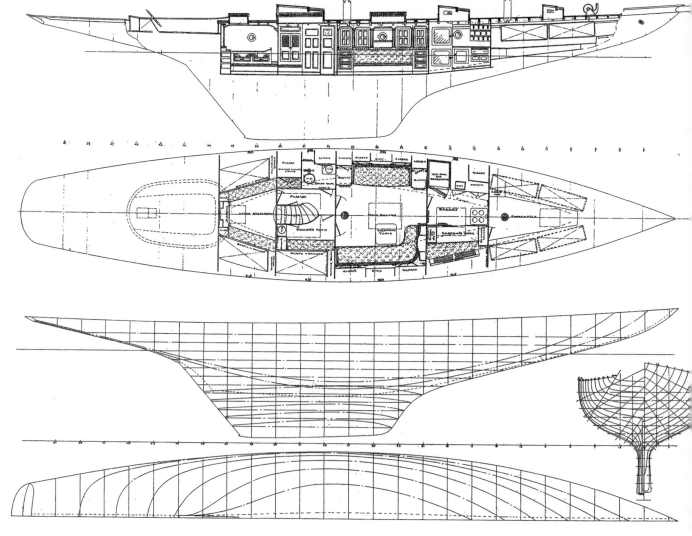

GAFF SCHOONER **ADVENTURESS**
OF 1913 BY B.B.CROWNINSHIELD

LOA	101'10"
LWL	71'2"
Beam	21'0"
Draft	10'6"
Sail Area	4,571 sq. ft.
Source	March 1913, pp. 245-46

Looking today almost exactly as she appeared brand new, **Adventuress** still operates on the West Coast. She's built fisherman fashion, with double-sawn frames, but the drawings show no keelson—generally considered to be a major structural member comprised of several layers sprung inside along the centerline after framing.

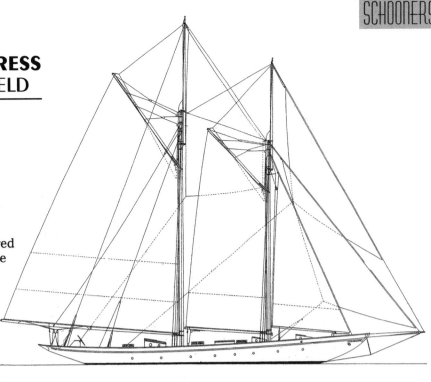

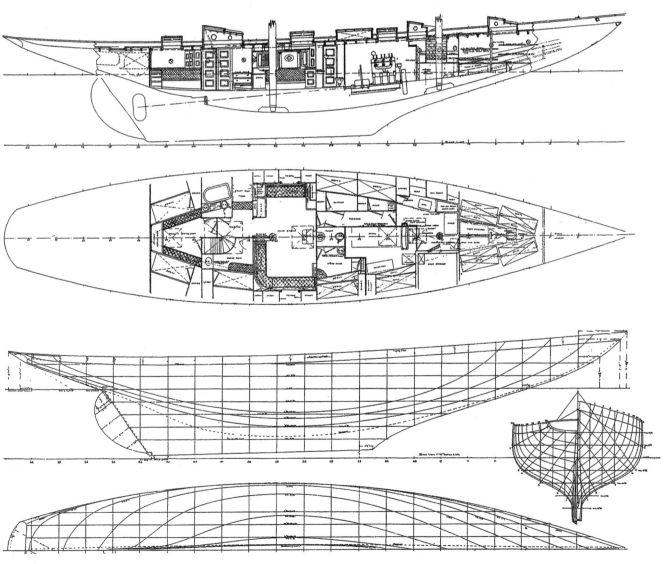

FISHING SCHOONER OF 1917
BY B. B. CROWNINSHIELD

LOA	126'0"
LWL	94'0"
Beam	25'0"
Draft	16'0"
Sail Area	6,468 sq. ft. (lowers only)
Source	April 1917, pp. 308-9

Once she arrived on the fishing grounds, her 16 dories would be dispatched, two men in each, to set out baited trawl lines for cod, while the schooner jogged nearby ready to later take aboard what each dory had caught. This was winter work and notoriously dangerous—the stuff writers loved to chronicle in newspapers, magazines, and books. No wonder these long, lean, and graceful hulls with towering rigs became legendary. This and nearly all the hundreds of other schooner-rigged, sailing fishermen were built at Essex, Massachusetts.

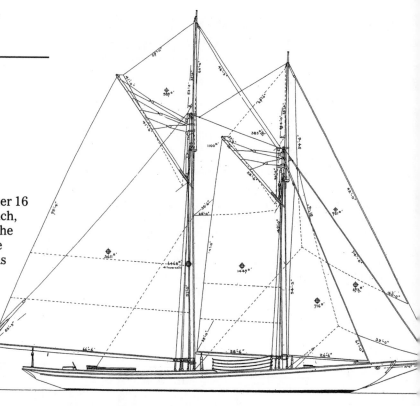

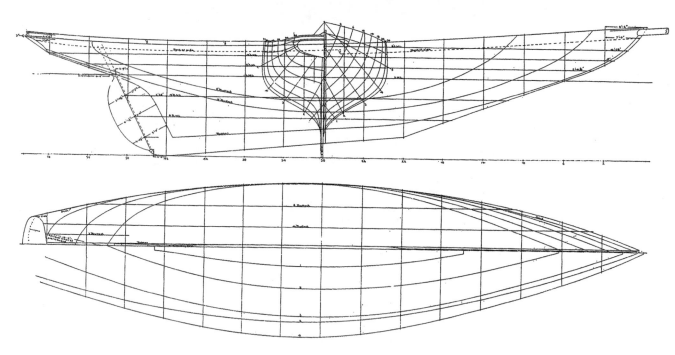

CARGO SCHOONER **PRISCILLA ALDEN** OF 1918 BY JOHN G. ALDEN

LOA	152'0"
LWL	142'0"
Beam	33'0"
Draft	12'6"
Source	January 1918, p. 32

World War I created a desperate need for cargo carriers and was responsible for the design and construction of several wooden coasting schooners, including this one. But the armistice had been signed before her launching, and within a few years she was converted to a yacht. In spite of a boxy shape for almost half her length, her bow and stern were sweetly modeled, and those ends along with the graceful sheer helped make a good-looking vessel instead of one that looked like a barge. These latter-day wooden vessels employed a substantial beam shelf instead of lodging knees to tie the deckbeams to the hull structure. This design also includes a propeller aperture and a shaftlog so that an engine could later be installed more conveniently. Frank C. Adams of East Boothbay, Maine, was the builder.

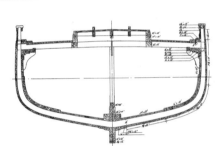

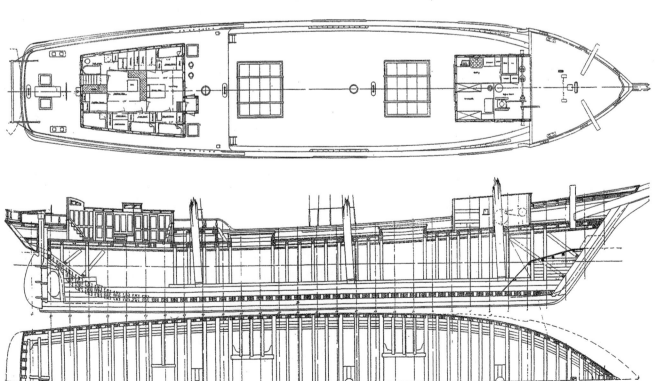

SAILBOATS

MOTORSAILERS

CAT-YAWL MOTORSAILER OF 1899 BY JOHN STUART & CO.

LOA	27′0″
LWL	23′0″
Beam	6′0″
Draft	2′4″
Source	April 1899, pp. 179-80

Branded with the name "auxiliary launch" because the term "motorsailer" hadn't yet been thought up, the hull of this craft does indeed look like a turn-of-the-century steam or naphtha launch. Without the rig, she'd be called a hunting cabin launch. She's included in this chapter, however, just to show that the idea of a combination motor-boat and sailboat has been around for longer than most people are aware of. She was very well built by her designers in Wollaston, Massachusetts, with copper rivet fastenings, white oak structural members, and cedar planking. For sleeping, if desired, the cabin settees could be slid together to form a single, large berth. The Alco-Vapor engine burned kerosene or coal oil instead of naphtha or gasoline, and its stack could be easily removed for sailing. Without a centerboard, this launch's shallow hull would make a good deal of leeway, close-hauled.

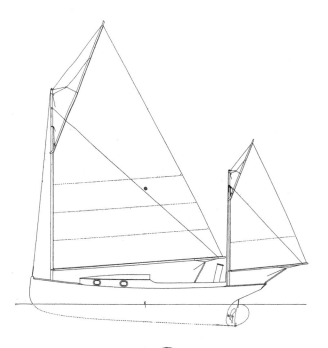

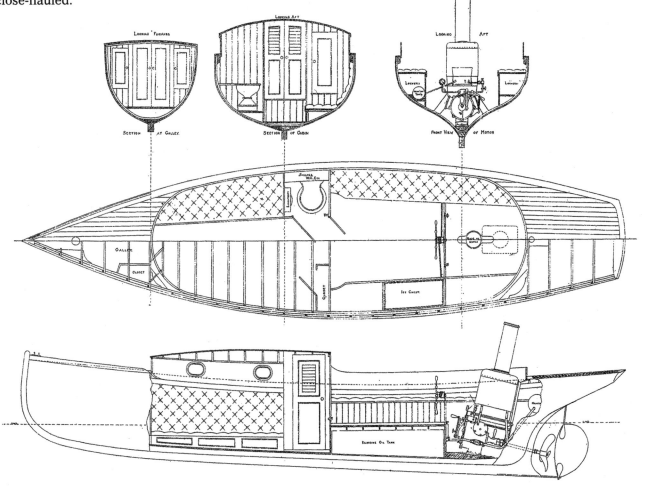

SLOOP-RIGGED MOTORSAILER OF 1929 BY HOWARD & MUNROE

LOA	35′0″
LWL	31′11″
Beam	9′0″
Draft	5′11″
Sail Area	690 sq. ft.
Source	March 1929, p. 86

Motorsailers were this era's discovery. Much was written about their virtues, and quite a number were built. Those designed by William Hand (see examples of his work on the following pages) were so numerous and so well publicized that his name was forever linked to the type. But other designers came up with intriguing creations as well, this being one fine example. She's more sail than motor, but with greater than the usual horsepower she'll drive along despite headwinds and seas. Access to that important power plant has been provided by a bulkhead door, one on either side of the companionway ladder. A raised foredeck and amidship trunk cabin provide over 6′ of headroom in both the main cabin and galley. (The sunken deck of the bow cockpit cuts into the height of the toilet room, however.) All in all, this is a pretty good compromise for what *The Rudder* describes as an "exceptional boat."

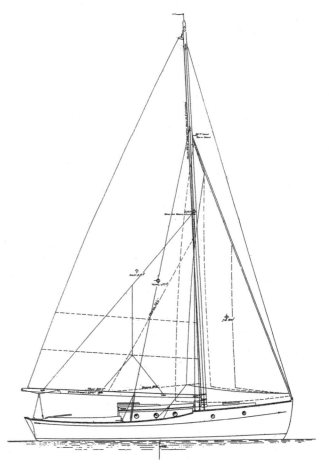

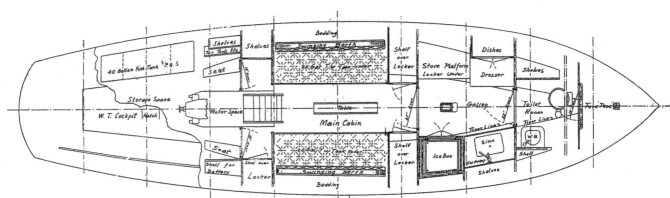

KETCH-RIGGED MOTORSAILER
CENTAUR OF 1929
BY JOHN G. HANNA

LOA	64′0″
Beam	16′7″
Draft	5′0″
Sail Area	1,074 sq. ft.
Power	150-hp Winton diesel
Source	November 1929, pp. 54-55

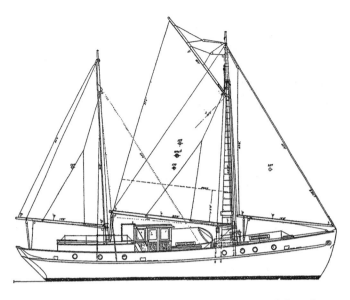

Using West Coast commercial vessels for inspiration and at his client's urging, Hanna came up with a design that is more motor than sail. A shallow hull of extra-heavy construction was also called for. The result is a husky craft with generous freeboard that looks as if it could deal in reasonable comfort with whatever weather she encountered— and a vessel that's pretty good-looking as well. The cabins run out to the rail for spaciousness, and the aft one can be entered from either the pilothouse or the cockpit. Open sleeping eliminates the usual staterooms in both cabins and becomes necessary, in some measure, because of the unusually large engineroom. For cruising the Bahamas, besides the shallow draft, **Centaur** has an outside steering station and ratlines up the mainmast to help in "reading" the water depth.

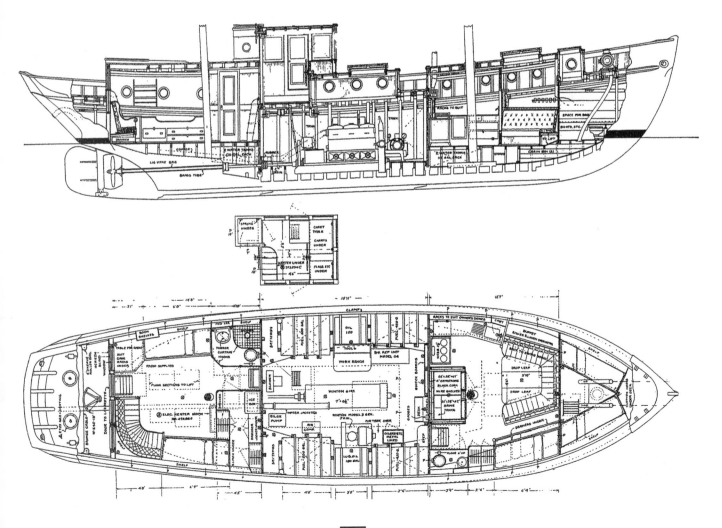

KETCH-RIGGED MOTORSAILER
BLUEBILL OF 1928
BY WILLIAM H. HAND, JR.

LOA	55′0″
LWL	46′11″
Beam	12′10″
Draft	5′0″
Sail Area	811 sq. ft.
Source	October 1928, p. 46

The narrow and raking fisherman stern makes **Bluebill** one of Hand's most graceful motorsailer designs. She's a development of Hand's previous yacht **Water Witch** and of the well-known and larger **Nor'easter.** The reason that Hand motor-sailers became so good so rapidly is that the designer himself always owned one, which he used extensively and thus came to know, first hand, how to improve his next design. Throughout all of Hand's work, the idea of a high bow and low stern prevailed.

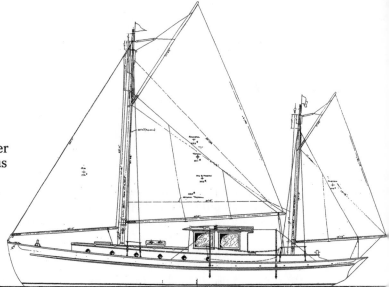

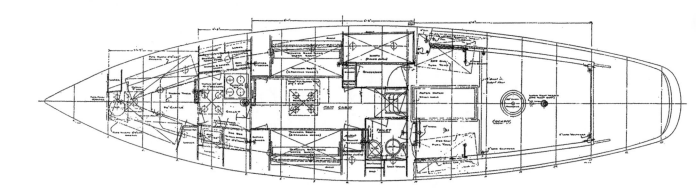

MOTORSAILER OF 1930
BY WILLIAM J. DEED

LOA 42'0"
Beam 10'4"
Power 25-hp Fairbanks-Morse diesel
Source February 1930, p. 70

Plainly built for cruising in the Pacific Northwest, this husky-looking craft would be adaptable for other climates. There's limited deck space, however. Motorsailers range widely in appearance. Some, like this, have rigs more to steady them from rolling than to propel them under sail with the engine shut down. In others, like the Howard & Munroe design a few pages earlier, sail is predominant. Deciding whether a motorsailer will be 50-50, 30-70, or 60-40 is only one of several basic parameters that have to be established early in the design process. In the hands of capable designers, good boats emerge no matter what the motorsailer trade-off. This boat is a good example; it's a design that will always be appreciated, no matter what the prevailing style.

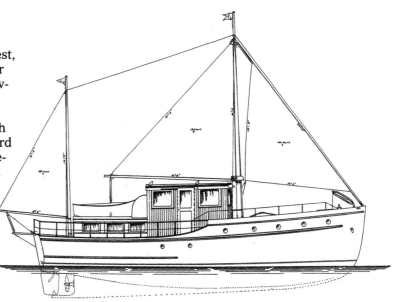

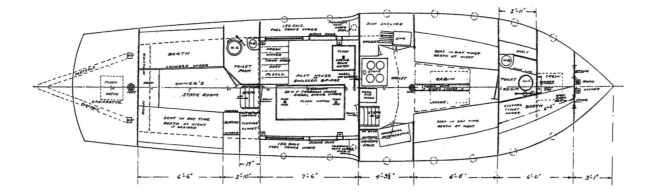

KETCH-RIGGED MOTORSAILER
OF 1934 BY WILLIAM H. HAND, JR.

LOA	47'7"
LWL	43'11"
Beam	13'8"
Draft	5'0"
Source	March 1934, p. 51

Wheeler Shipyard of Brooklyn, New York, a yard known for its standardized power cruisers, commissioned motorsailers in four sizes from designer Hand, of which this is next to the largest. There's an aft cabin for the owner, and the usual main cabin, toilet room, and galley forward of the open-backed pilothouse. As you can see, there's not much usable deck space—only the mostly roofed-over cockpit—so this is not a craft for sun worshipers. But for all the room below, she's still handsome and would make a practical cruiser in damp climates like the Pacific Northwest.

SLOOP-RIGGED MOTORSAILER
BUCKEROO OF 1935
BY WILLIAM H. HAND, JR.

LOA	51'8"
LWL	50'1"
Beam	14'5"
Draft	4'10"
Displ.	56,000 lbs.
Power	100-hp Hall-Scott gasoline engine
Source	July 1935, p. 41

Hand's later motorsailers like **Buckeroo** became finer lined, wider, and shallower—but by no means excessively so. A simpler, single-masted rig showed up as well. Hodgdon Bros. of East Boothbay, Maine, was by this time Hand's favored builder and built **Buckeroo** for his personal use. Hand invariably called for a small sleeping cabin for himself near the pilothouse, while his guests slept in the main cabin and the hired man in his own quarters in the fo'c's'le. R. O. Davis actually drew most all the plans during Hand's motorsailer era (1927-40) and gradually assumed the role of co-designer. Davis's perspectives, two of which show here, allow easy visualization of portions of the interior. Unlike the previous, mostly closed-in 48-footer, **Buckeroo** has loads of usable deck space.

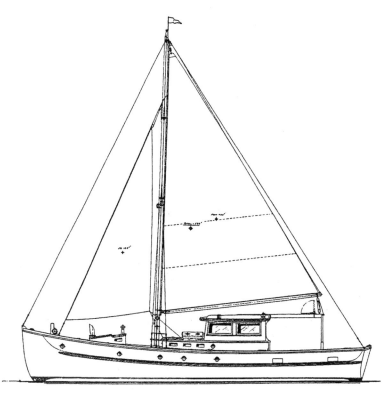

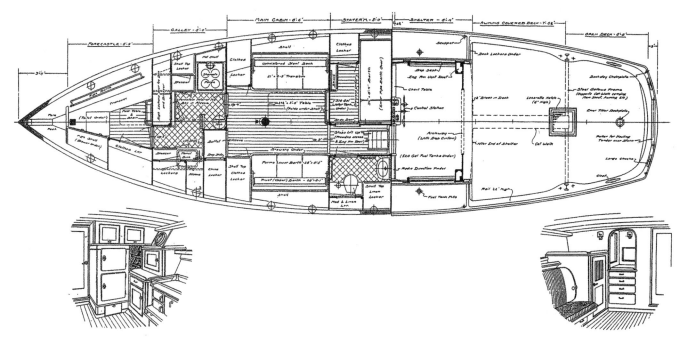

POWERBOATS

LAUNCHES & RUNABOUTS

FANTAIL LAUNCH OF 1899
BY JOHN STUART & CO.

LOA	26′0″
LWL	22′9″
Beam	5′11″
Draft	2′2″
Source	December 1899, pp. 448-50

A decent set of lines drawings for the once ubiquitous fantail launch are rare indeed, but by using this boat's profile, deck plan, and the three construction sections, one could develop lines for a nice-looking craft of this type. She is shown with one of the compact Alco-Vapor engines—a unit that burns kerosene and uses vaporized alcohol inside the cylinders themselves in an expansion, condensing, and heating cycle similar to that of a steam engine. A naphtha engine is similar in size and shape but used a single liquid (naphtha)

instead of two. The engine operator sat in this launch aft of a paneled bulkhead, while the passengers enjoyed the view from the cockpit forward of that same bulkhead. The Stuart company claimed that their launch could be adapted to any make of engine, but it's obvious that an Alco-Vapor, naphtha, or gasoline engine would fit in better than even the smallest steam plant. (Another similar-sized Stuart launch is featured in the motorsailer chapter.)

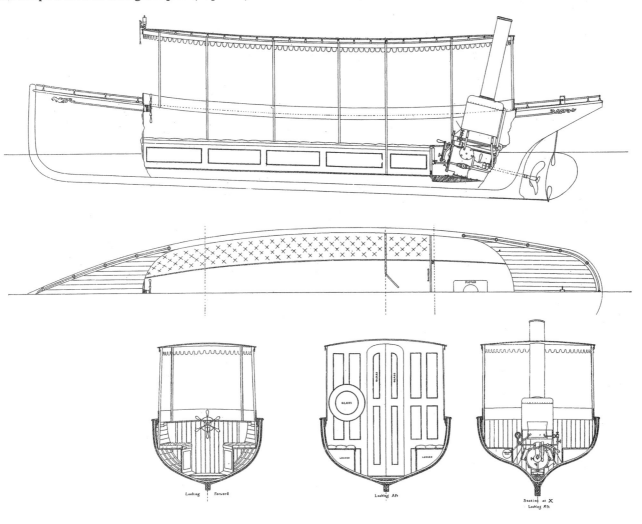

FANTAIL LAUNCH OF 1900
BY FRANK NICHOLS

LOA   22′4″
LWL   18′3″
Beam   5′4″
Draft   1′7″
Source April 1900, pp. 182-83

Here's a smaller launch with a curved and raking stem that may be not so striking but is still useful in understanding the classic launch's hull shape—especially its fantail stern. A 3- or 4-horsepower gasoline engine is the recommended power, and, as you can see, it lies at the aft end of the cockpit.

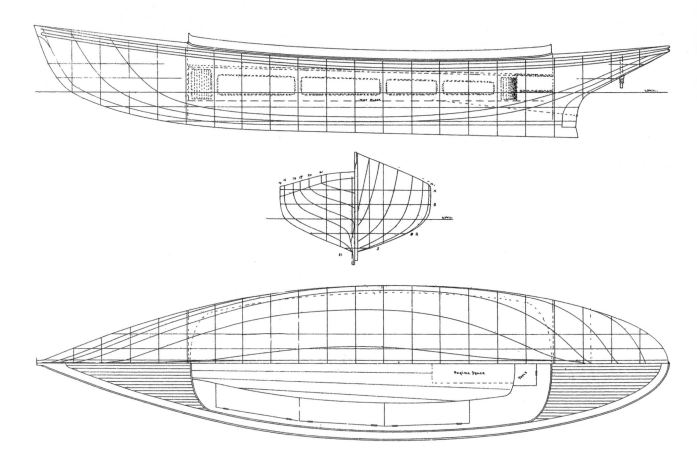

POWER DORY **BONITO** OF 1904
BY CHARLES D. MOWER

LOA 18′0″
Beam 4′10″
Draft 1′3″ (at skeg)
Source May 1904, pp. 305-9

Power dories like this and larger, because they were so cheap to buy and easy to build, were favored over the more traditional, round-bottomed launches. *The Rudder* ran this power dory as a complete how-to-build feature with dimensioned drawings and written instructions. She'd be amazingly simple to build (only five planks per side and four sawn frames), and, as dories go, she'd be stable as well. The bottom board is heavy (1″ oak), and there's generous beam at the waterline. A typical, one-lunger engine is shown for power, but builders today may want to consider one of the small self-contained, air-cooled four-cycle gasoline engines made by Honda or Briggs & Stratton.

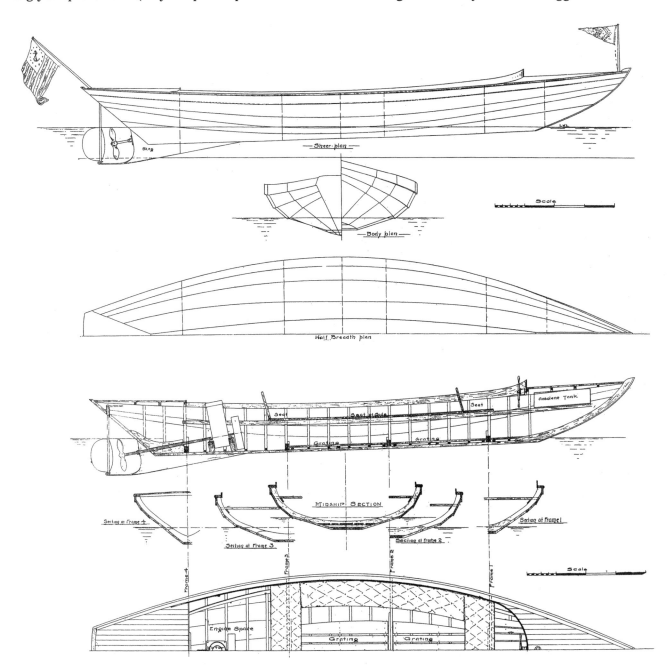

POWER TENDER OF 1904
BY WILLIAM J. J. YOUNG

LOA	14′0″
Beam	4′0″
Draft	1′2″
Source	May 1904, p. 325

Quite like a Whitehall rowboat in shape and size, but somewhat wider and more burdensome, pretty little boats like this, fitted with single-cylinder engines and known as power tenders, found use as towboats for the unpowered sailing yachts they tended. They also served as shore boats, shuttling the owner and his guests between the moored yacht and a shoreside landing. Provisions for hoisting were always part of the outfit, and, as you can see, this design includes a davit iron attached to the keel forward, and a hanger strap attached to the back side of the towing bitt aft. Although not shown, chances are she had stick steering along one side or the other, with steering chains attaching to the stick partway up its length. Not only is this an appealing little craft, but designer Young has included all the necessary building information on this single drawing.

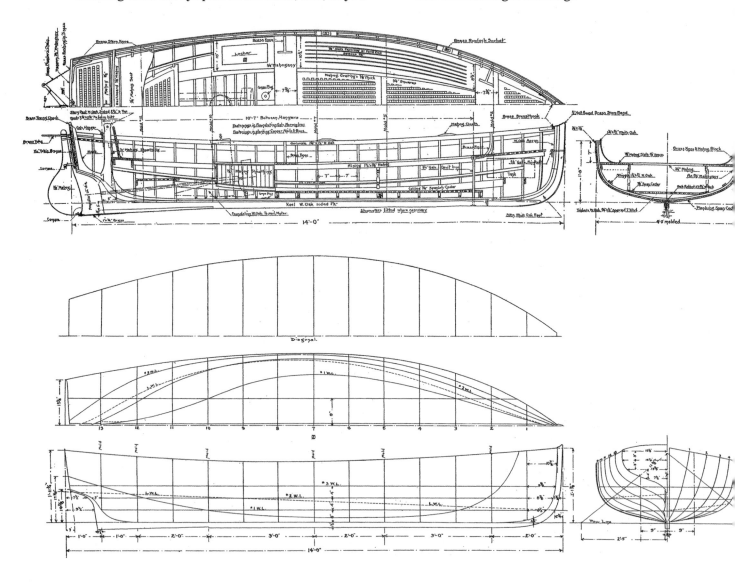

DOUBLE-ENDED LAUNCH OF 1908
BY CHARLES D. MOWER

LOA	25′0″
LWL	21′6″
Beam	7′0″
Draft	2′3″
Power	10-hp Mianus gasoline engine
Source	September 1908, p. 168

Waters surrounding Fishers Island (at the eastern end of Long Island Sound) include The Race and other current-troubled areas known for their steep, close-together wave formations that at times challenge small boats in a big way. Knowing this launch would be used there, owner H. C. Cushing and designer Charles Mower agreed that she should have greater beam and more freeboard than was the custom in 1908, and be of the proven, seaworthy double-ender hull shape. The engine was placed under a hood to keep it dry, and the boat decked over for much of its length as protection against taking solid water aboard. The dry storage area under the aft deck can be reached through a lockable hatch. Huntington Mfg. Co. of Huntington, New York, built this pretty little launch.

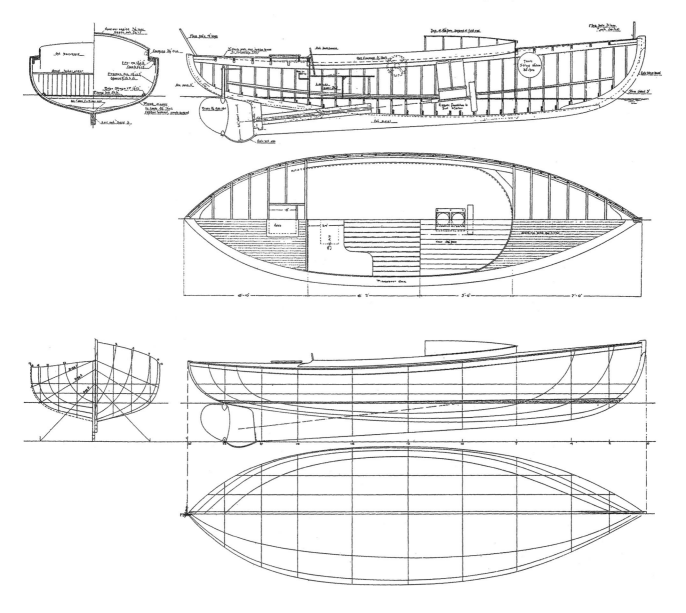

LAUNCH **ECHO** OF 1909
BY PALMER BOAT CO.

LOA	27' 1"
LWL	25' 10"
Beam	6' 6"
Draft	1' 5"
Power	4-cylinder Jencick gasoline engine
Source	January 1909, p. 46

Tumblehome at the stern and a trace of flare near the bow give this launch the character that many of her contemporaries lacked. Launches laid out like this, with the engine under a hood and forward of a bulkhead, and with an auto-type steering wheel, were often called "autoboats." The motor car and motorboat businesses blossomed together in response to rapidly improving gasoline engines, and the Midwest became a spawning ground for this dual evolution. **Echo** was built in Fontana, Wisconsin, by her designers.

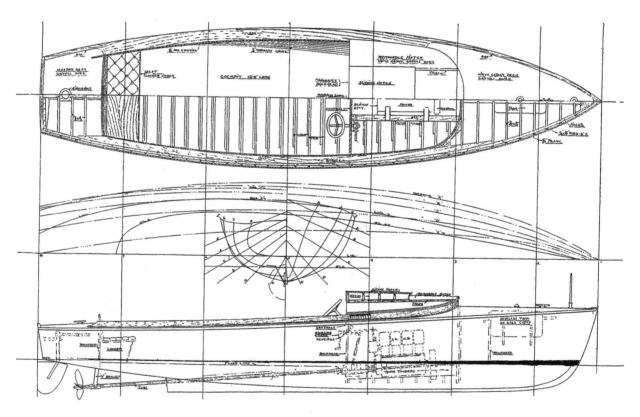

GASOLINE CABIN LAUNCH **OTTO**
OF 1897

LOA	53'0"
Beam	9'0"
Draft	4'6"
Power	25-hp Otto gasoline engine
Source	September 1897, pp. 255-56

Cabin launches, or "glass" cabin launches as they're often called for obvious reasons, at first contained steam engines and boilers and coal and all that went with such a power plant. Whereas those yachts had precious little space left over for the crew and passengers, the same hulls became serious cruisers when powered by a compact gasoline engine. As you can see here, there's a crew's cabin aft of the engine and nice, long settees forward of it, as well as a couple of settee/berths in the pilothouse. **Otto** could sleep seven, according to *The Rudder*. Her hull is a kind of stretched-out version of the Alco-Vapor fantail launch shown at the beginning of this chapter.

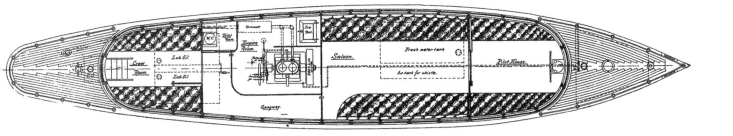

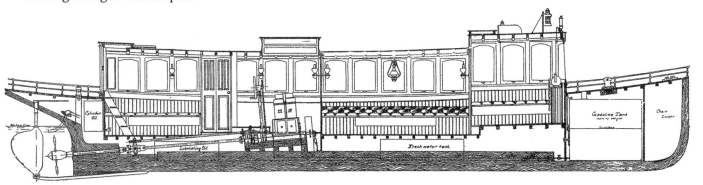

DOUBLE-ENDED CRUISING LAUNCH OF 1901 BY CHARLES D. MOWER

LOA	60′2″
LWL	57′6″
Beam	11′2″
Draft	3′10″
Displ.	39,040 pounds
Power	30-hp Wolverine gasoline engine
Source	March 1901, pp. 102-5

This design predates the term power cruiser, so boats like this were called cruising launches. Built for cruising the Gulf waters surrounding New Orleans, this well-thought-out cruiser was built in Grand Rapids, Michigan, by The Wolverine Motor Works and made the run home on her own bottom via the Mississippi River. Her engine, a product of the yard that built her, is boxed-in in the galley and its top forms a table for the chef. As you can see by the several section views, the cabin structure essentially forms a box within the confines of the hull, with settees that run along both sides with but few interrup-

tions. There's a ladies' room aft of the galley with suitable hanging lockers, drawers, and a bureau with mirror. The toilet room, complete with bath-tub, can be entered either from the ladies room or through a sliding door from the galley. The awning-shaded cockpit has no built-in seats, but is designed to accept turn-of-the-century rattan chairs. For sleeping, all the settees pull out to make them wider. There's no door shown in the pilothouse, but there must have been some means of gaining access to the deck besides through the ladies' room.

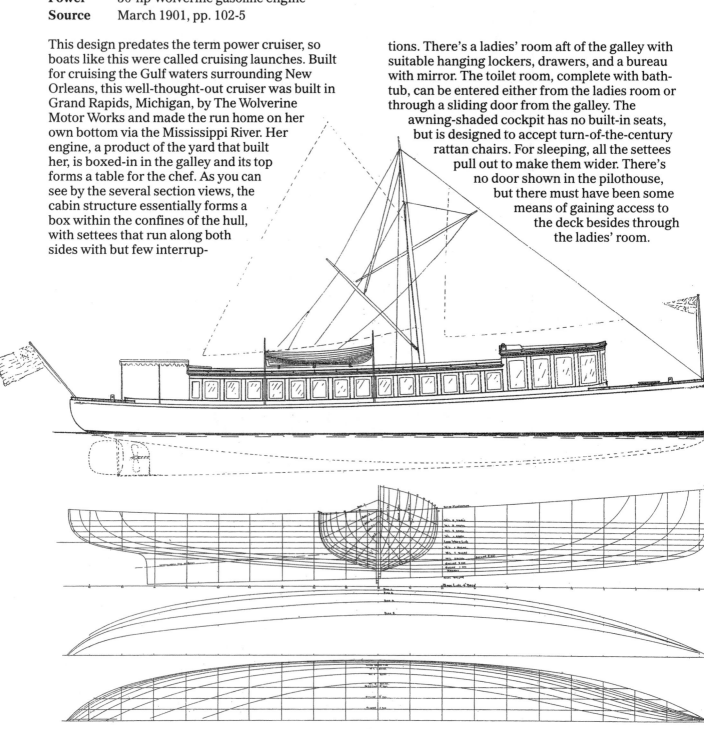

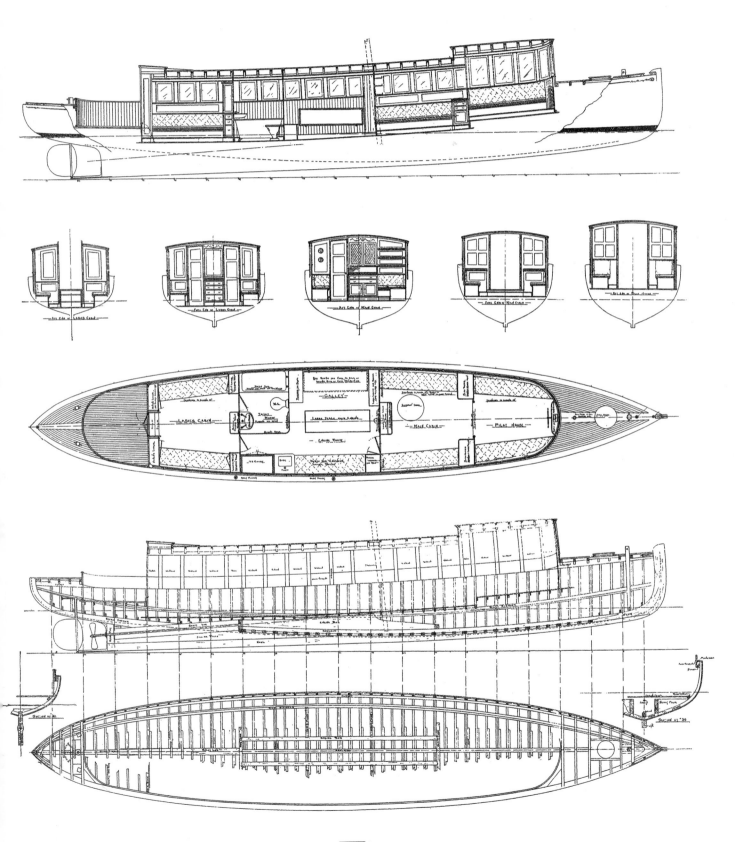

DOUBLE-ENDED CRUISING LAUNCH OF 1903 BY H.C. TOWLE

LOA	50′ 0″
LWL	47′ 0″
Beam	14′ 0″
Draft	2′ 6″
Power	20-hp, 3-cylinder gasoline engine
Source	November 1903, pp. 570-71

For its day, this was a very wide yacht whose designer was one of the first to realize how accommodations benefit from greater beam. As with the previous launch, sleeping is on the settees but in this case additional width comes from swing-down backs as well as pull-out extensions. Night-time curtains form two separate sleeping cabins and the desired privacy. The aft cabin on this yacht is the engineer's domain where the engine remains completely exposed. The cooking is done here as well. The rattan chairs would have to be up on deck, since this launch has no cockpit whatsoever, but the owner and his family or guests might prefer to stay inside anyway, just to soak in the ambiance that all the lovely joinerwork creates. Even the steel arch that strengthens the hull amidships is sheathed with coved-out wood. Too bad the lines drawing wasn't published, but just from the arrangement drawings—especially the sections—one can judge this to have been a handsome craft.

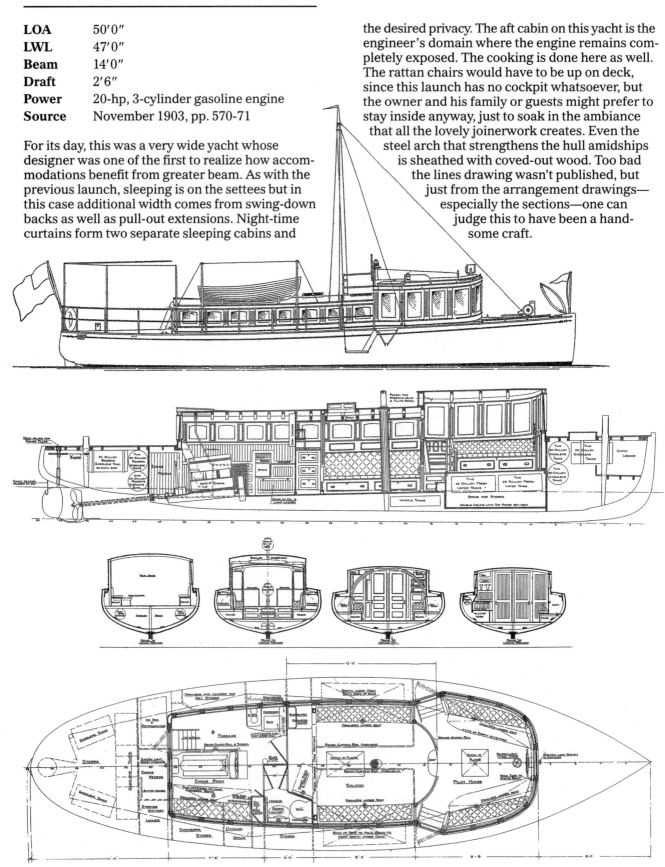

STERN-WHEELER LAUNCH
ALLIGATOR OF 1911
BY R. M. HADDOCK

LOA	42′ 3″ (including paddle wheel)
LWL	33′ 2″
Beam	8′ 11″
Draft	9″
Power	20-hp 3-cylinder gasoline engine
Source	May 1911, pp. 389-94, and June 1911, pp. 461-66

This craft was too intriguing to pass up. Her obvious advantage is shallow draft and the ability to churn along in weed-infested water without fouling the driving mechanism. She's a smooth-water craft for sure, and even with her three rudders would be a handful to steer when it's rough and windy. Headroom at 5′ 4″ is a little scant, but you increase it only with a corresponding increase in windage—maybe not a good idea. *The Rudder* published the designer's very detailed instructions as well as his detailed drawings in a two-part article, so even a rank amateur has a chance.

Alligator is really a big, flat-bottomed skiff with an unusual propulsion mechanism at the stern. Might make an interesting project, or at least serve as inspiration for one.

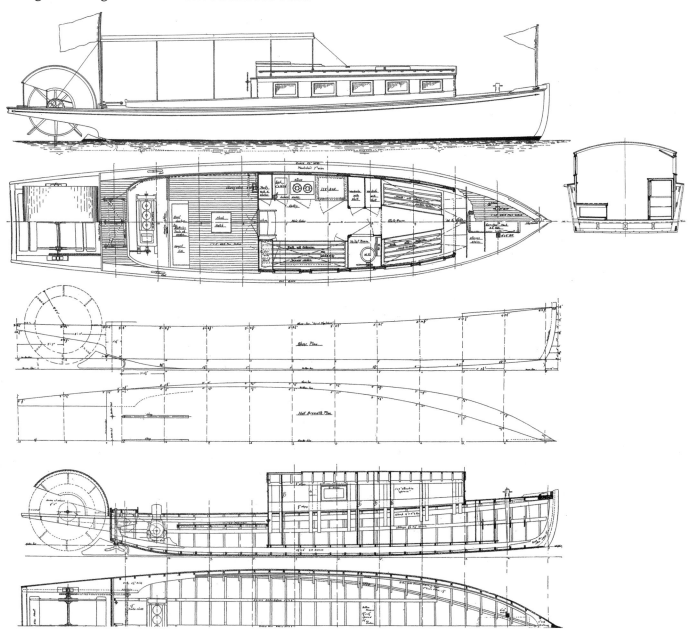

DOUBLE-ENDED CRUISING
LAUNCH OF 1905 BY F. D. LAWLEY

LOA	86′6″
LWL	79′6″
Beam	14′0″
Draft	4′8″
Power	Two, 4-cylinder Standard naphtha engines
Source	May 1905, pp. 315-17

A bow thruster would help this yacht in close quarters, as the twin propellers are too close together to assist much in turning. Nevertheless, she's a handsome craft in which one could cruise comfortably. In this yacht, the place to be by day is either in the pilothouse forward or the saloon (main cabin) aft. At night, the place of choice would be the stateroom because of its built-in berths, although the settees elsewhere convert to berths for less private sleeping. For the paid crew there are pipe berths under the pilothouse sole and no doubt other amenities in the fo'c's'le not shown on the drawings. Geo. F. Lawley & Son of South Boston was the builder.

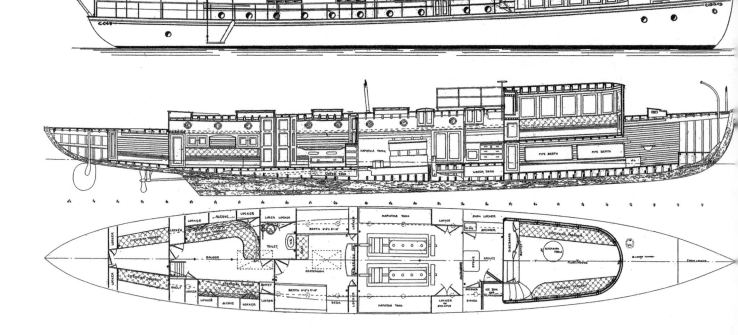

CABIN LAUNCH **DAWN** OF 1916
BY BOWES & MOWER

LOA	50′0″
LWL	46′0″
Beam	12′0″
Draft	4′0″
Power	60-hp Lamb gasoline engine
Source	January 1916, pp. 13-16, and March 1920, pp. 14-16

This boat's power plant goes beyond the above stated gasoline engine in that it includes a generator and an electric propulsion motor as well. The resulting gasoline-electric drive was an experiment of owner William T. Donnelly, who saw promise in adapting what he could learn from **Dawn** and her sister **New Era** to a commercial tug-and-barge operation. The idea was that the surplus electrical power generated aboard the tug (**Dawn**, in the experiment) would be transferred by means of an electrical cable to the barge (**New Era**) to drive its electric propulsion motor. (**New Era** had no engine and only limited battery power.) Great publicity surrounded these experiments, one of which consisted of **New Era** actually leading **Dawn** up the Hudson and back again. The cable hookup appears vulnerable, but the pair of launches were lovely little things, well equipped with cruising accommodations.

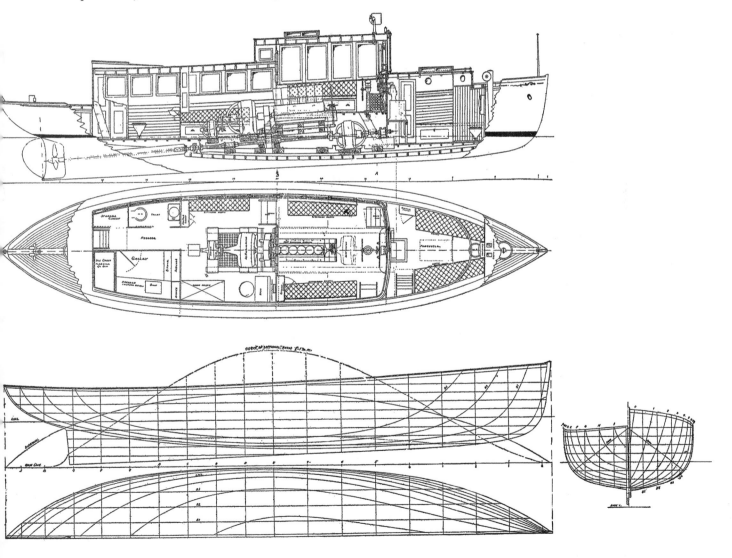

YACHT CLUB LAUNCH OF 1930
BY FORD, PAYNE & SWEISGUTH

LOA	30′0″
LWL	29′2″
Beam	8′3″
Draft	2′3″
Power	25-hp 2-cylinder Palmer gasoline engine
Source	June 1930, p. 57

By the 1930s, launch proportions had reached the peak of their development, or nearly so. Length-to-beam ratios had diminished to 3 or 4 to 1, and flaring bows and more buoyant sterns prevailed. With out becoming much heavier, engines underwent vast increases in horsepower, which, in turn, allowed boats to be pushed beyond their natural hull speed. While not able to fully plane, boats like this one, although shorter and fatter than earlier launches, could attain the same speed. Club launches shuttled yachtsmen and their families and guests between their moored yachts and the yacht club float. They'd board the launch from the yacht's starboard side, so the port side of the launch was arranged to receive or discharge passengers.

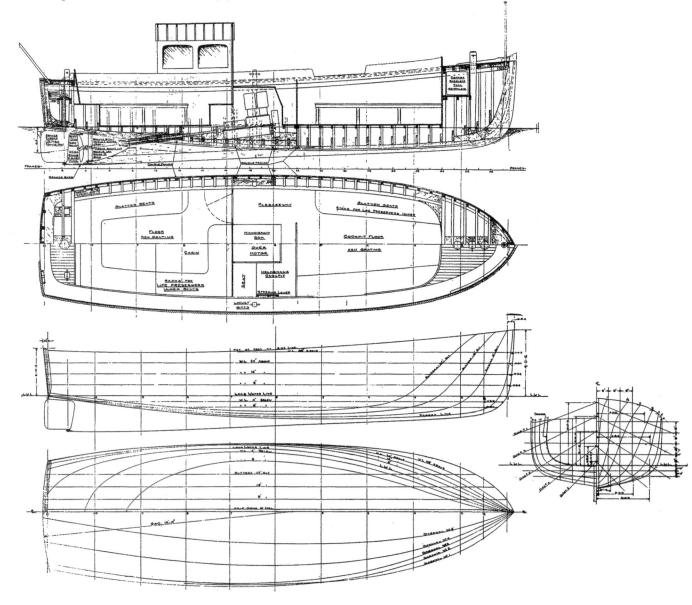

RAISED-DECK RUNABOUT **PIUTE III** OF 1912 BY WILLIAM H. HAND, JR.

LOA	24′0″
Beam	5′6″
Draft	1′0″
Power	30-hp 4-cylinder Loew-Victor gasoline
Source	October 1912, p. 183

Speed distinguishes a launch from a runabout. This one would do 20 miles an hour wide open, with her bow in the air and planing. V-shaped forward sections kept her from pounding in rough water, and, unlike many of her contemporaries, **Piute III** is said to have been exceptionally dry and seaworthy. **Old Glory**, an owner-built boat of this same design, made the open-water passage from Long Island Sound to Yarmouth, Nova Scotia, and returned safely and in reasonable comfort. (*Motor Boating* magazine for December 1912 and January 1913 describes this adventure.) Hand's V-bottomed runabouts, of which there were many, became immensely popular in the years before the Great War, and a number besides **Old Glory** were owner built.

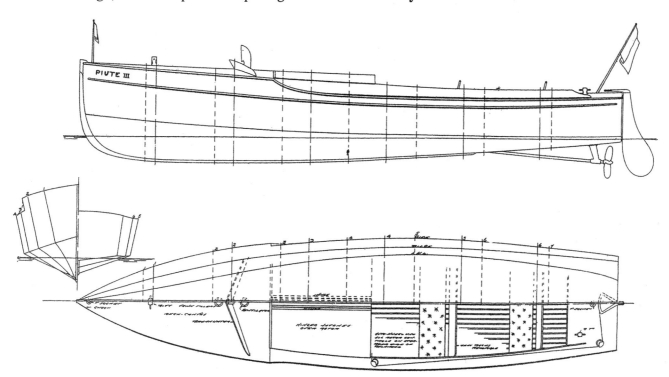

TWO-COCKPIT RUNABOUT OF 1909 BY B. B. CROWNINSHIELD

LOA	32'0"
LWL	30'8"
Beam	4'9"
Draft	1'3" (at skeg)
Power	24–28-hp 4-cylinder Jencick gasoline engine
Source	April 1909, p. 393

With an "autoboat" layout, this Hodgdon Bros.-built craft could do 16 or 17 miles an hour, according to the writeup in *The Rudder*. You'd have a wet ride in a seaway because of the low freeboard and lack of buoyancy forward, but that's part of the overall thrill. The extreme tumblehome at the stern, along with the reverse-raked V-shaped transom, are a part of the era's style.

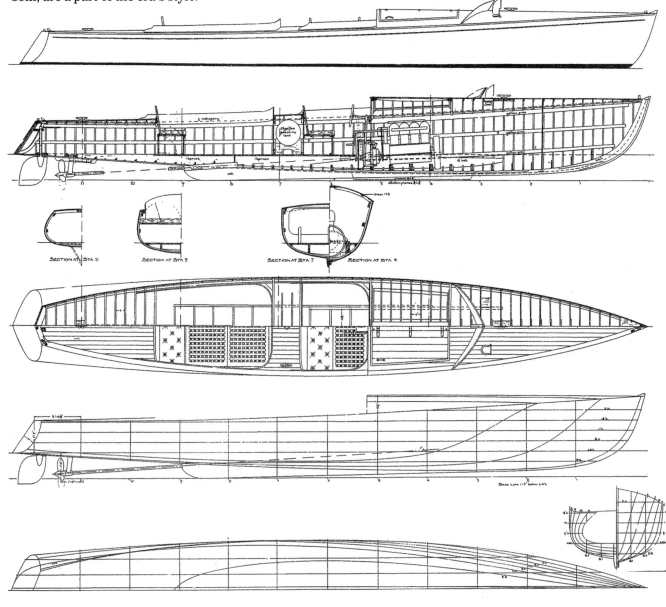

FAY & BOWEN RUNABOUT OF 1913
BY MORRIS M. WHITAKER

LOA	32′0″
Beam	5′6″
Power	30–45-hp Fay & Bowen gasoline engine
Source	January 1913, p. 29

Here's another runabout best suited for relatively calm water. She'll do a little over 20 miles per hour. Although her autoboat layout is typical for the era, the treatment of the engine hatch and coaming are particularly attractive. This was a standardized offering from the Geneva, New York, based Fay & Bowen Engine Co., which not only built gasoline engines but also many of the boats that used them.

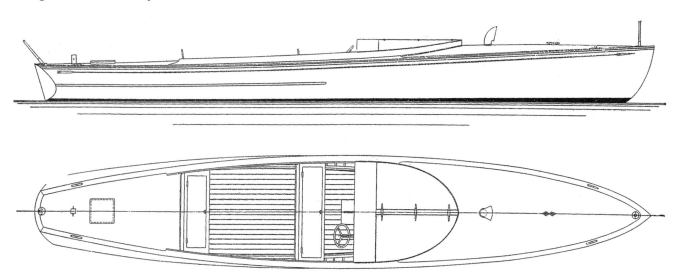

SEDAN YACHT TENDER OF 1927
BY CHRIS-CRAFT

LOA	22′0″
Beam	6′0″
Power	Chrysler Imperial gasoline engine
Source	September 1927, p. 63

Chances are that this boat would be hoisted out on a yacht's davits when the yacht was underway, and lowered into the water to serve her primary purpose when the yacht anchored. She's much like a runabout but for the shelter cabin over the aft cockpit where the privileged yachtsmen sit. Although Chris-Craft sold many more standardized boats than any other manufacturer, it's rare to find published plans in the yachting magazine design sections. But the Chris-Craft archives, including the plans, have survived and are one of The Mariners' Museum's most active collections.

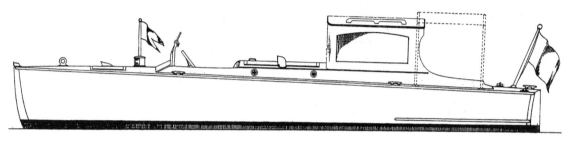

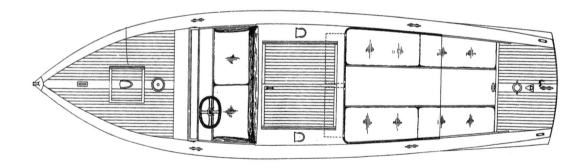

YACHT CLUB LAUNCH OF 1918 BY A. E. LUDERS

LOA	32'0"
Beam	8'0"
Power	10-hp Palmer gasoline engine
Source	February 1918, p. 53

Even a small cabin like this provides a distinctive look, especially in a boat without much sheer or freeboard. This cabin exists primarily for shelter, with looks being secondary. It was where one sat to get out of the wind, rain, and spray. Youngsters, of course, always favored the open forward cockpit. In season, club launches like this scurried about the anchorage, busily ferrying passengers to and from their yachts, and occasionally towing fleets of sailboats to the starting line and back home again after they finished racing. Chances are that the rope fender rail shown here was supplemented in some manner with additional padding, so as not to risk scraping the topsides of the yachts being tended. This boat was designed for the Stamford (Connecticut) Yacht Club and was elegantly built by Luders Marine Construction Co. of the same city.

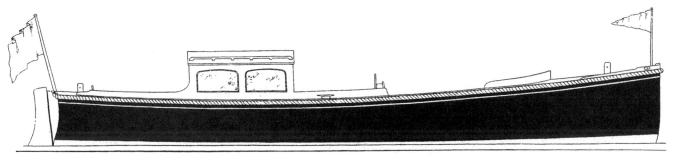

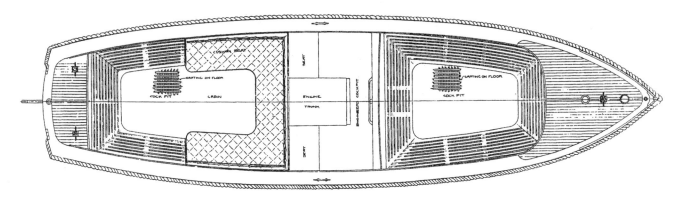

POWERBOATS

POWER CRUISERS & MOTOR YACHTS

CLIPPER-BOWED POWER CRUISER
NOKOMIS OF 1903
BY MARTIN C. ERISMANN

LOA	75'6"
LWL	62'0"
Beam	14'0"
Draft	3'8"
Power	Two 25-hp Standard gasoline engines
Source	May 1905, pp. 324-25

The Marine Construction & Drydock Co., of Staten Island, New York, built **Nokomis** in 1903 for W. S. Van Clief, who had cruised some 1,800 miles in her before *The Rudder* published these drawings. She's especially attractive, and with the beautiful clipper bow and raking stack looks more like a steam yacht than one powered by gasoline. Below deck, curtains were relied upon to shut off various areas at night for sleeping. **Nokomis** carried a four-man crew who slept next to the engines and adjacent to the galley, one man being the engineer and another the cook; a professional captain and steward probably made up the rest of the crew. Like many power yachts of her day, **Nokomis** carried steadying sails on both masts to minimize rolling in a beam sea.

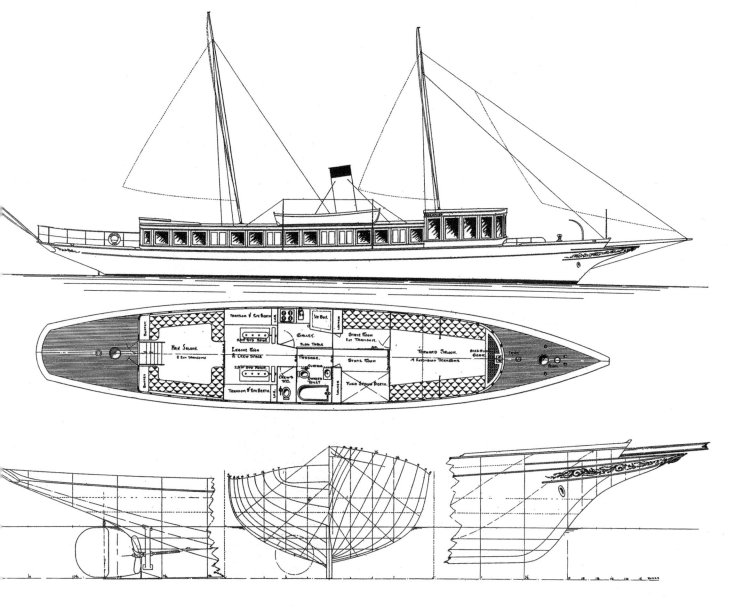

ROUND-STERNED FISHING BOAT **PIONEER** OF 1913 BY JOHN G. ALDEN

LOA	48'6"
LWL	42'3"
Beam	11'6"
Draft	4'4"
Source	February 1913, pp. 76-77

Contemporary commercial vessels served as the basis for **Pioneer**'s design which, because Alden proportioned her so nicely, gives one the impression of a vessel half again her size. To look well, the pilothouse has been sunk so its sole is below the main deck level. This cuts into the headroom under it, so that's where the engine has been placed. In this yacht's layout, the crew also sleeps next to the engine, which encourages them to keep it clean and in perfect running order. The aft half of the yacht is for the owner and his family and friends.

There are two staterooms, a main saloon that can be converted for sleeping at night, and the usual bureaus and lockers. As the plans indicate, **Pioneer** was a very sweet-lined vessel.

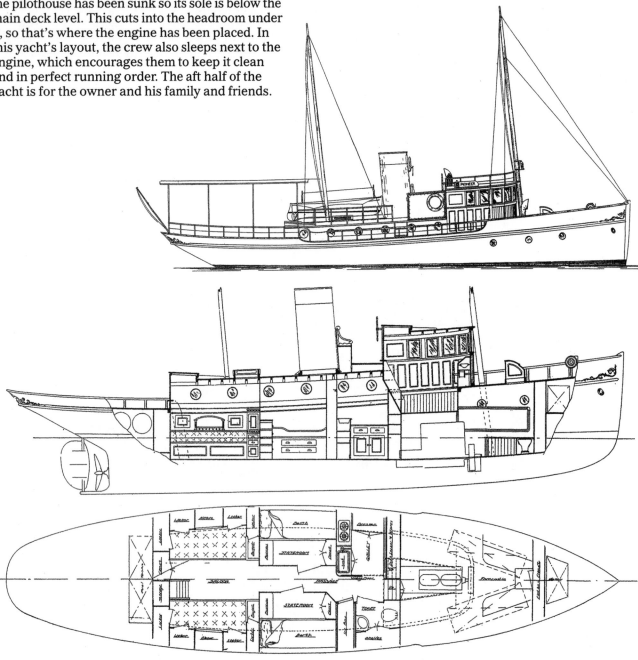

POWER CRUISER OF 1914
BY BOWES & MOWER

LOA	46'6"
Beam	11'0"
Draft	3'3"
Power	3-cylinder Standard gasoline engine
Source	July 1914, pp. 358-59

A low profile and lots of tumblehome at the stern sets this design apart from most of the others. Although it's possible to make the trip from the forward stateroom to the main cabin without going on deck, the usual route would have been via the deck so as to avoid passing through the engineroom, crew's quarters, and galley. Steering is very much in the open and must have been wet at times, although at least some of the spray was thrown aside by the flaring bow. The steering cable is completely accessible, as it runs from the quadrant (under the grating aft) to the steering wheel. The stack, made large for a better appearance, is functional nevertheless and serves both for the engine exhaust and the galley stovepipe.

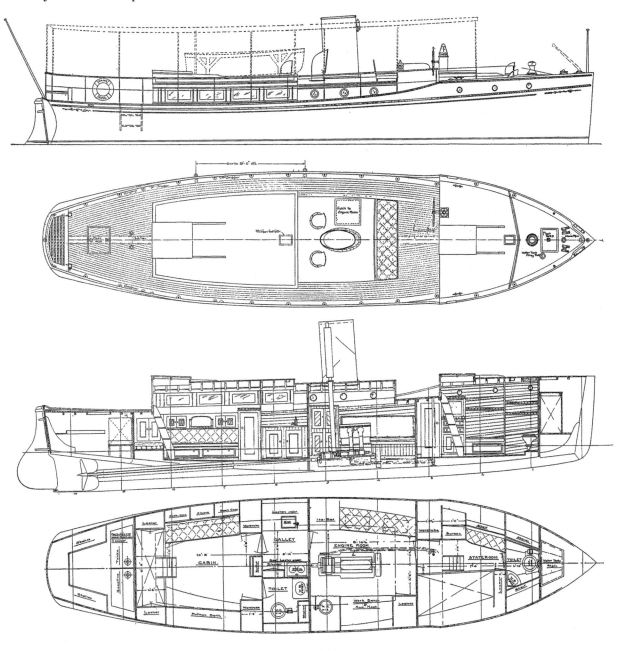

V-BOTTOMED, RAISED-DECK POWER CRUISER **PORPOISE** OF 1916 BY FREDERICK W. GOELLER, JR.

LOA	28'0"
Beam	8'6"
Draft	2'8"
Source	May 1916, p. 235, June 1916, p. 287, July 1916, p. 330, & August 1916, p. 375

Porpoise, designed specifically for *The Rudder*, came out as a four-part how-to-build article. Goeller's fine eye created a nice-looking craft from characteristics that generally produce a boxy one: a V-bottom, high freeboard, and a raised deck. Goeller gave her sides a little curve, with some flare forward, while at the stern there's tumble-home and a transom that's slightly V-shaped. A touch of carved scrollwork at the bow, combined

with a full-length cove cut in just below the sheer guard, also help push the design above the average. A self-bailing cockpit is rather unusual here, but is a way of getting the gasoline tanks out of the bilge and any leakage or spillage around them to drain directly overboard.

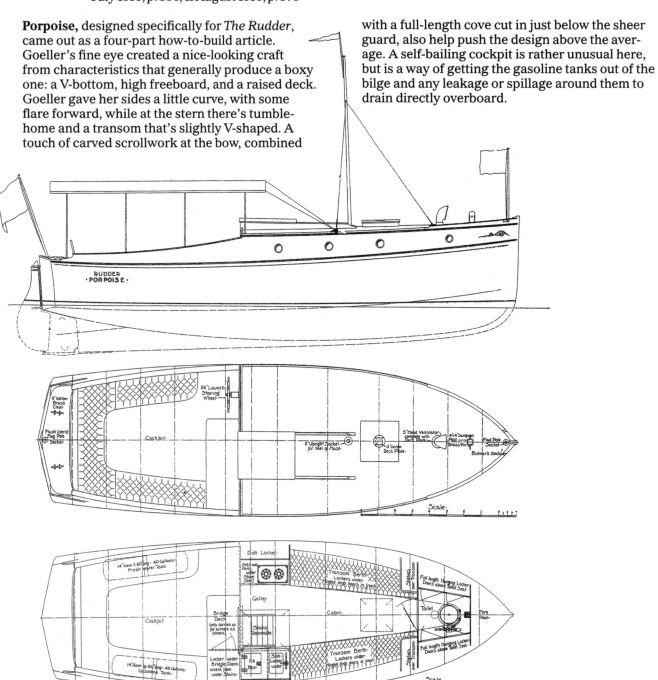

MOTORYACHT L'APACHE
OF 1914 BY CONSOLIDATED SHIPBUILDING CORP.

LOA	72′0″
LWL	71′6″
Beam	12′0″
Draft	3′6″
Power	Two 125-hp Speedway gasoline engines
Source	December 1915, pp. 527-28

At the time of **L'Apache**'s October launching, the designer/builder's complete name was Gas Engine & Power Co. and Charles L. Seabury, Consolidated, later to be shortened simply to Consolidated. From this Morris Heights plant, located on the Harlem River at the northern tip of Manhattan, came some wonderful power yachts in great abundance and all with a distinctly recognizable style. 'Midship

pilothouses with lots of glass were among their familiar features. Although an early example, **L'Apache** was no slouch; her guaranteed speed was 19 miles an hour.

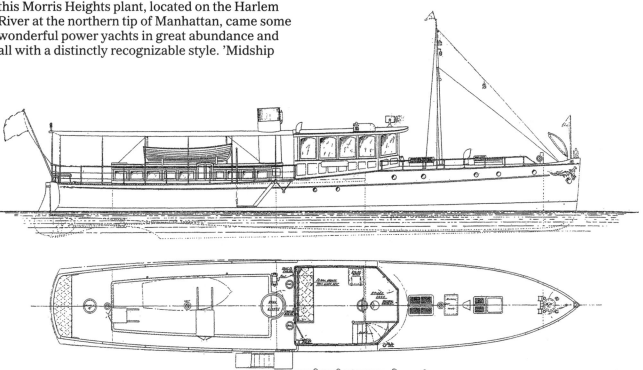

POWER CRUISER **PEG O' MY HEART** OF 1917 BY F. S. NOCK

LOA	67'0"
LWL	66'0"
Beam	13'0"
Draft	4'0"
Power	4-cylinder Standard gasoline engine
Source	September 1917, pp. 607-10

Only a few designs are drawn so that all their principal dimensions come to even feet, and this is one of them. Whether by intention or by accident it's hard to say, but in any event, Nock produced a good-looking design. The sole of the forward deckhouse has been placed below deck level for the sake of appearance, but it's still possible to enjoy the view while seated—an important consideration in any yacht. The cook, however, whose galley is located in the aft port corner of this deckhouse, stands four steps lower and is deprived of any such view. The helmsman stands on deck to steer, and just behind him in front of the vestigial smokestack there's a settee where those who choose to "take the air" can sit on pleasant days. Besides being a designer, Nock was a builder with a yard in East Greenwich, Rhode Island, and that was where **Peg o' My Heart** was constructed.

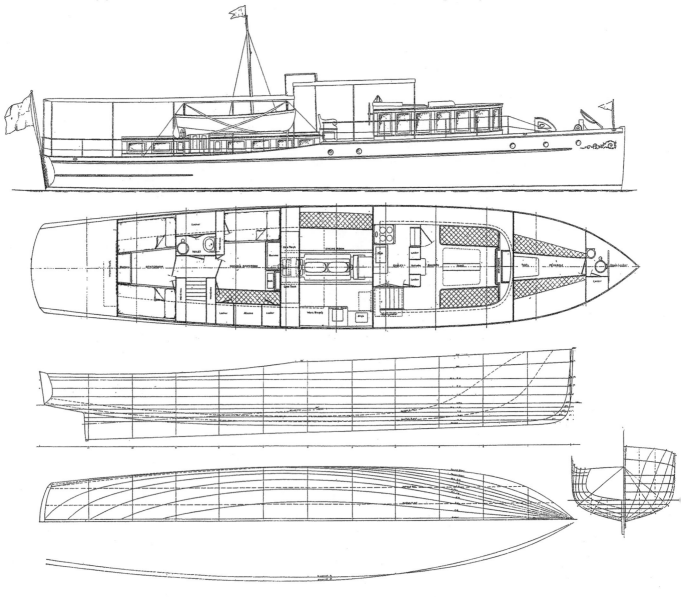

SHALLOW-DRAFT, RAISED-DECK POWER CRUISER OF 1918 BY COX & STEVENS

LOA	54'6"
LWL	53'6"
Beam	12'0"
Draft	1'11"
Power	Two 50–60-hp Speedway gasoline engines
Source	May 1918, pp. 244-46

To quote from *The Rudder*, "Mrs. Ballard [the owner's wife] drew the plans for the interior arrangement and these show in a remarkable way a woman's ingenuity for utilizing all space for closets and storage....Mrs. Ballard's apartments are in the forward part of the boat...aft of [the galley] is a cabin for Mr. [S. Thurston] Ballard's use." A yacht this size would normally draw a foot or two more water, but shallow draft was one of the stated parameters of this design. Thus, she was given the necessarily small propellers and tiny rudder, and no drag at all to the keel profile. Cox & Stevens produced a remarkable craft for the intended sheltered-water use, but one that would do rather poorly offshore.

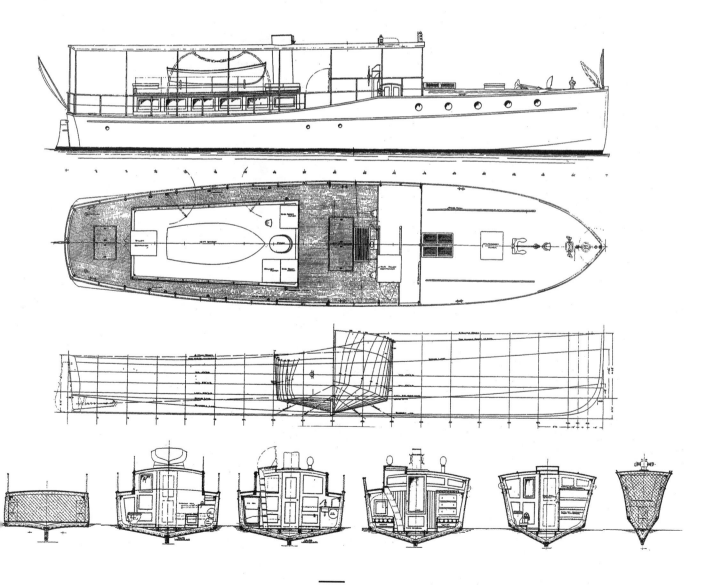

HOUSEBOAT **MIMI B II** OF 1922 BY NEW YORK LAUNCH & ENGINE CO.

LOA	67'0"
Beam	17'0"
Draft	3'6"
Power	Two 6-cylinder Twentieth Century gasoline engines
Source	June 1922, p. 27

Houseboats gained popularity with the opening of the intracoastal waterway, because they made wonderful liveaboards in which Northerners could enjoy Florida's winter warmth. Big and boxy as a general rule, a few houseboats, like **Mimi B II**, looked quite good. This one's raised deck, graceful sheer, and moderately sized deckhouse enhance her overall looks. Carved scrolls and a covestripe help as well.

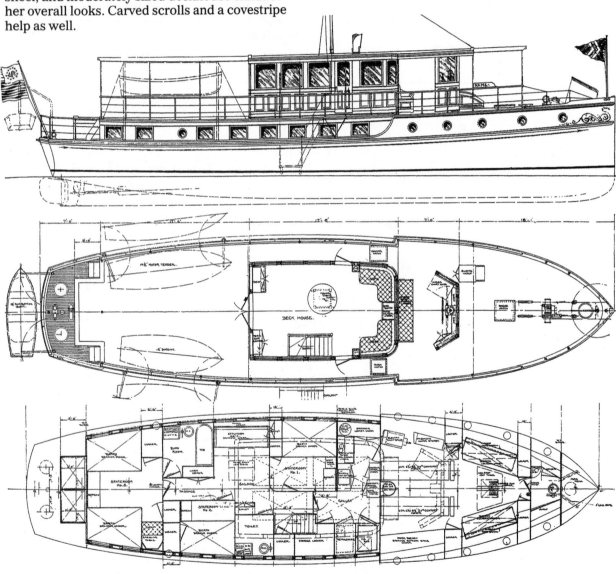

HOUSEBOAT OF 1929
BY PHILIP L. RHODES

LOA	55′0″
Beam	18′0″
Draft	3′0″
Power	Two six-cylinder Gray gasoline engines
Source	December 1929, p. 60

Besides being a dozen feet shorter than **Mimi B**, this houseboat's arrangement is very different. The crew's quarters and enginerooms are aft instead of forward, there's a huge main saloon amidships, steering takes place within the deckhouse, and the three staterooms are placed up forward. Working within the constraints of full headroom and shallow draft, designer Rhodes produced a decent-looking boat within an overall length that's really too short for her type.

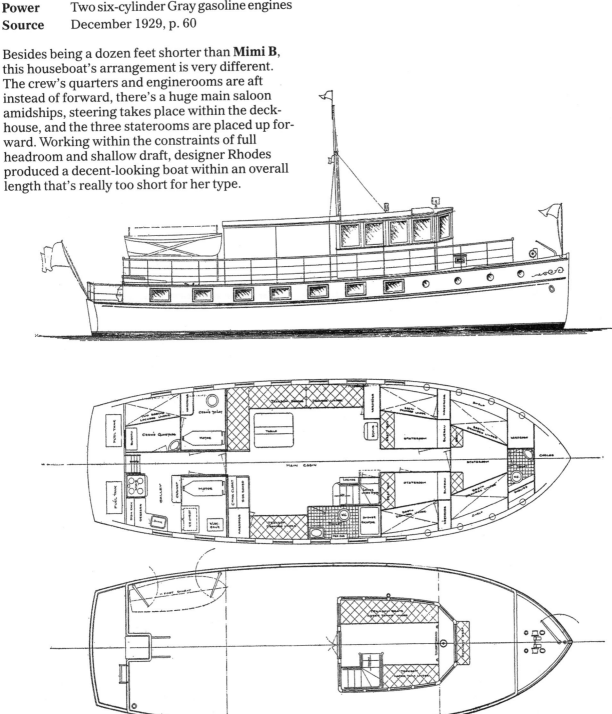

POWER CRUISER **VENTURE II**
OF 1923 BY B.T. DOBSON

LOA   35'0"
Beam   9'6"
Power 30-hp Lathrop gasoline engine
Source December 1923, p.25

By observing moderation in all respects, Dobson turned out this unusually handsome power cruiser, with a round-front trunk cabin, an unbroken sheerline, a wineglass-shaped transom, and pretty rudder outline. Of note below decks are the quarter berths that run aft under the cockpit, and the forward placement of the galley. There's no way of knowing what the pilothouse's front windows looked like, but if they followed the attractive appearance of what shows in the profile drawing, **Venture II** would have been lovely to view from any angle.

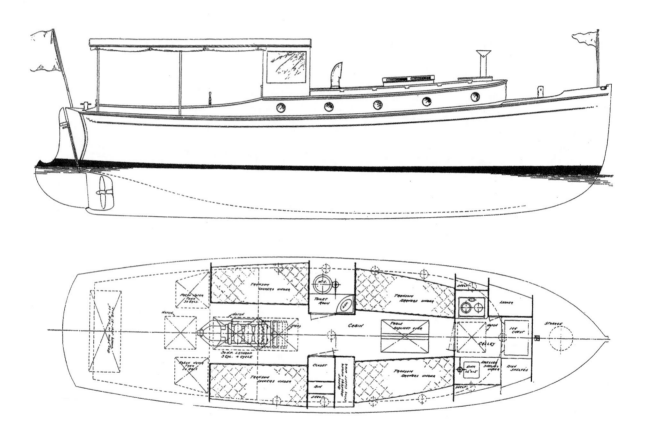

RAISED-DECK POWER CRUISER
MARYBELLE II OF 1925
BY FRANCIS SWEISGUTH

LOA	49′10″
LWL	49′6″
Beam	10′6″
Draft	3′3″
Power	180-hp Speedway gasoline engine
Source	March 1925, pp. 48-49

Narrow side decks make for a hazardous outside passage between the cockpit and steering station and may not have been used much, especially with the cockpit awning in place. (Chances are that most traffic took place below deck through the lobby and saloon.) But the benefit of such a feature is more space in the saloon, toilet room, and galley. Not a bad trade-off, considering the boat's narrow beam. The plumb stem, together with minimal cabin structure, gives **Marybelle II** a businesslike appearance.

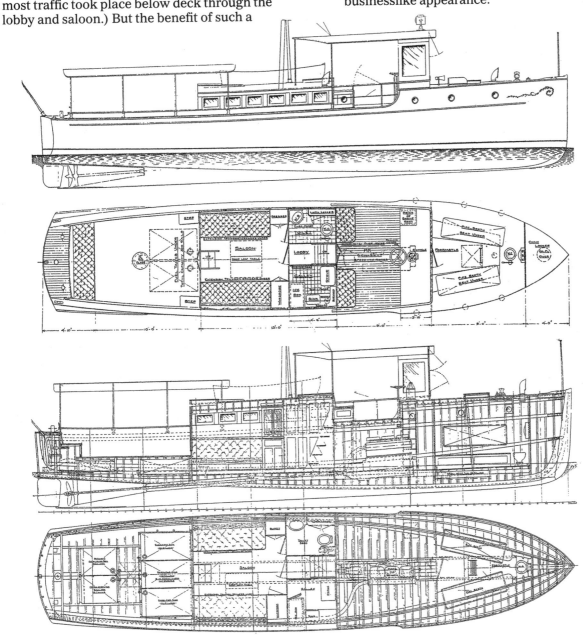

RAISED-DECK POWER CRUISER
SUMJOY OF 1926
BY S. S. CROCKER, JR.

LOA	36'6"
LWL	36'0"
Beam	10'6"
Draft	3'0"
Power	35-hp Kermath gasoline engine
Source	September 1926, pp. 40-41

Crocker designed mostly sailboats, but had no problem at all drawing plans for graceful, practical, and shippy-looking powerboats like **Sumjoy**. His treatment of what happens at the break of the deck is especially interesting. While the raised deck appears to end abeam of the mast, the headroom below continues at almost full width four more frame bays to where the pilothouse ends, creating enough extra space for the galley including a cou-

ple of lockers as well as two sizable opening windows. The full deckline forward means there's considerable flare—harder to build, but nice to look at—and there's some tumblehome aft to complement the flare. The recessed deck for anchor handling and the generous skylights atop the main cabin are great features as well. B. W. Rand of Boothbay Harbor, Maine, was the builder.

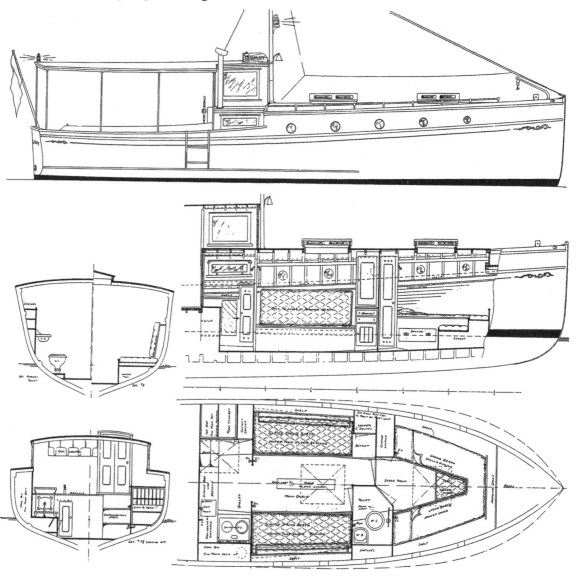

POWER CRUISER **ELEANOR III**
OF 1926 BY S.S. CROCKER, JR.

LOA	51'0"
Beam	13'0"
Draft	3'6"
Power	Two 65-hp Kermath gasoline engines
Source	December 1926, p. 52

Here's a larger Crocker design of the same general type as **Sumjoy** and also a shippy-looking craft, built by Falmouth Foreside Yacht Yard, Falmouth Foreside, Maine. Dining is where the view is best—right up in the big-windowed pilothouse—the galley adjacent, a half-level below. Guests enjoy the convenience of going to their quarters directly after boarding through the entrance opposite the starboard gangway. Two double staterooms, each with its own skylight but sharing the same tub-equipped toilet room, are located within. For those who enjoy watching astern at the vanishing wake, there's a built-in settee on the aft deck under the shade of the awning.

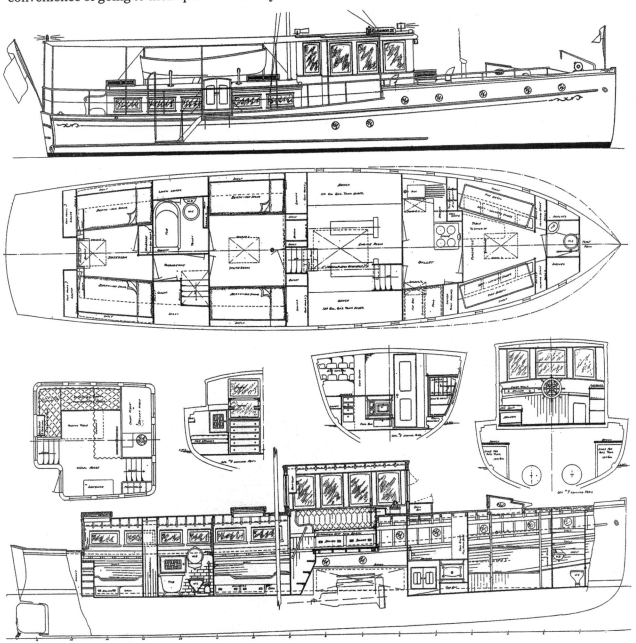

RAISED-DECK POWER CRUISER OF 1927 BY CONSOLIDATED SHIPBUILDING CORP.

LOA	45′0″
Beam	11′6″
Draft	3′3″
Power	180-hp Speedway gasoline engine
Source	February 1927, p. 55

The tiny aft cabin and cockpit arranged for sport fishing are the two unusual features to be noticed immediately in this design. The seat atop the aft cabin is another. From this perch, one gets a fine view of passing scenery even forward because of the big pilothouse windows. There's lots of deck space on board, with most of it sheltered by the canvas awning. Side curtains can be unfurled for inclement weather.

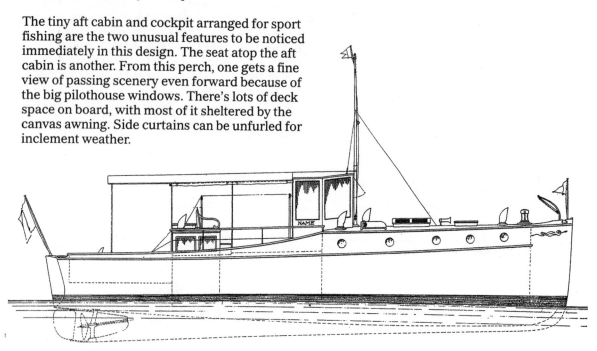

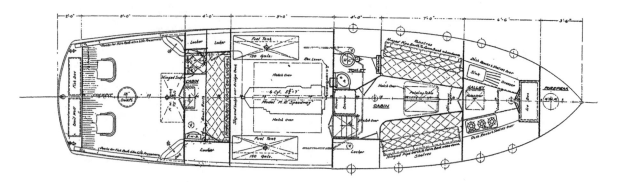

EXPRESS CRUISER **ROBALISS III** OF 1926 BY CONSOLIDATED SHIPBUILDING CORP.

LOA	73′0″
LWL	70′9″
Beam	12′6″
Draft	3′6″
Power	Two 300-hp Speedway gasoline engines
Source	August 1926, p. 55

There's nothing like length in a boat to ease the task of creating a beautiful design. Here's an example. With that gorgeous, unbroken sheer, even the big-windowed pilothouse looks okay. Consolidated's two basic arrangements for yachts of this type were with the owner's quarters forward and the crew's aft, as in **Robaliss**, or the other way around. In either layout, the sunken deckhouse was owner territory, used for entertaining and dining. The forward cockpit lent itself best to the arrangement shown here since its location placed it directly adjacent to the owner's stateroom.

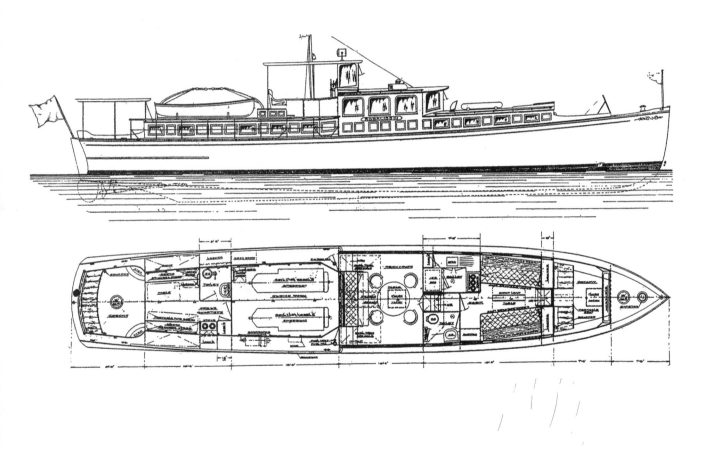

COMMUTER **CIGARETTE**
OF 1928 BY JOHN H. WELLS

LOA	75′1″
LWL	74′2″
Beam	12′11″
Draft	4′0″
Power	Two 450-hp Winton gasoline engines
Source	November 1927, p. 53

Cigarette, similar to **Robaliss III** on the previous page, features a sheltered aft cockpit adjacent to the owner's quarters and a raised foredeck with another cockpit near the bow. This handsome yacht, owned originally by L. Gordon Hamersley, was recently acquired by the International Yacht Restoration School of Newport, Rhode Island, in derelict condition and now awaits a complete restoration. She's worth it, having been beautifully built by Henry B. Nevins, Inc., City Island, New York.

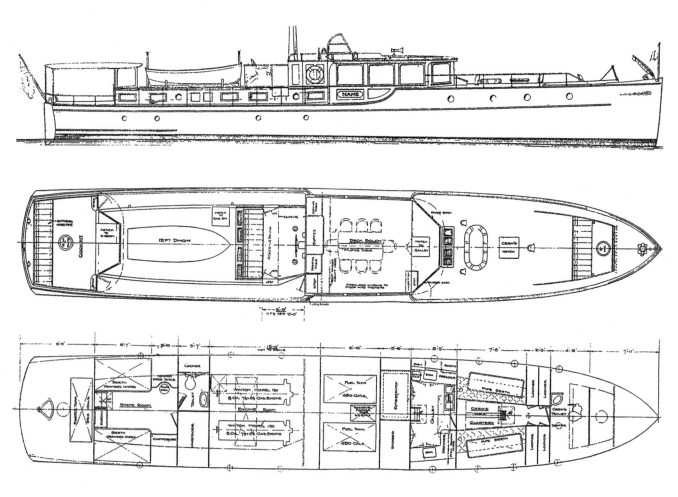

MOTORYACHT SCOUT OF 1925
BY JOHN H. WELLS

LOA	85′0″
LWL	81′6″
Beam	17′0″
Draft	5′9″
Power	Two 100-hp Winton gasoline engines
Source	November 1926, p. 41

No matter whether you're lounging on the fantail, enjoying the view forward from the on-deck settee, or inside the windowed deckhouse, life aboard **Scout** would be most enjoyable. You can even choose whether you'll dine at deck level or below, since there's a table on both levels. The two winding stairways, one forward and the other aft, make it easy and convenient to pass from one level to the other. A davit-hung owner's launch rests atop the deckhouse when the big yacht is underway, and at such times the boarding platform would be hoisted clear of the water as well. She's a stately, seagoing yacht, although with only 100 horsepower driving each of her propellers, she's obviously not a fast one. **Scout** was German built by Lurssen Yacht & Bootswerft in Vegesack.

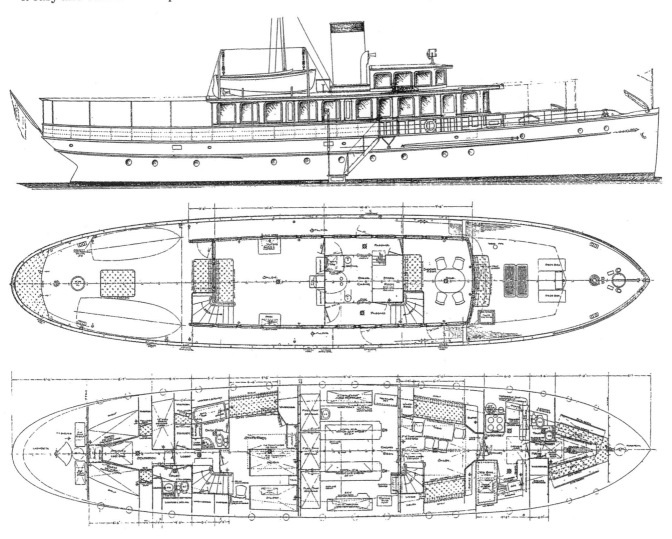

CREATIONAL FISHING BOAT
SKUNK OF 1928 BY A. E. LUDERS, SR.

LOA	55'11"
LWL	54'0"
Beam	11'3"
Draft	3'0"
Power	Two 6-cylinder Sterling Dolphin gasoline engines
Source	April 1928, p. 49

Owner Philip L. Smith had a lovely waterfront summer cottage in Tenants Harbor, Maine, so he had no need for a cruising power yacht. (Any local cruising would be done in his gaff sloop **Dyon** shown in the sloop chapter.) **Skunk**, appropriately painted black and white just as shown here, was a day boat designed for occasional deep-sea fishing at the mouth of Penobscot Bay—thus the large, self-bailing cockpit. She'd do about 25 miles an hour, so getting there and back didn't take long. And one could steer from the forward cockpit where the engine and exhaust noise was minimal and the visibility superb.

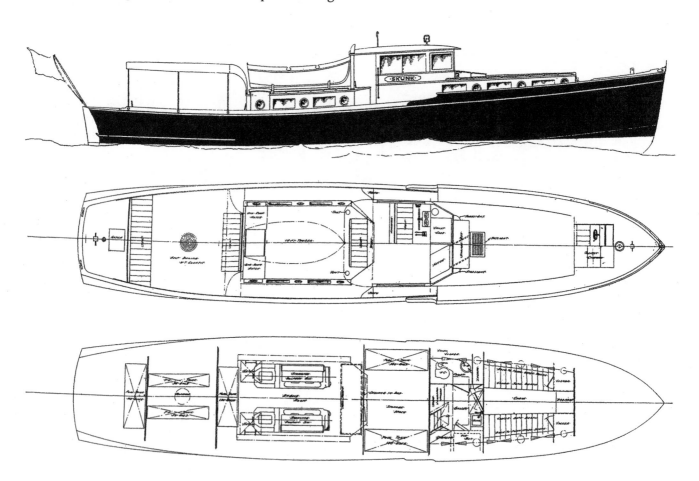

MOTORYACHT **SEA DREAM**
OF 1925 BY A. E. LUDERS, SR.

LOA	99'11"
LWL	97'9"
Beam	17'4"
Draft	5'0"
Power	Two 6-cylinder Sterling Viking engines
Source	March 1925, p. 43

Luders depicted most of his designs with black hulls, making them distinctive for their era. (Sparkman & Stephens later adopted this same technique.) But when launched from the designer's Stamford, Connecticut, yard, many

Luders yachts, including **Sea Dream**, were painted white. By alternating rectangular windows with round portholes Luders gave his creations a unique character, regardless of the hull color. Except for the forward half of the sunken deckhouse which is set up for dining, the owner's and guest accommodations are aft of the engineroom, terminating in a sheltered aft cockpit. **Sea Dream**'s low profile is a popular carryover from the naval vessels of the First World War.

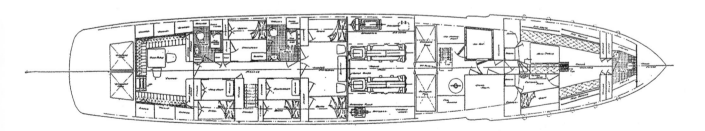

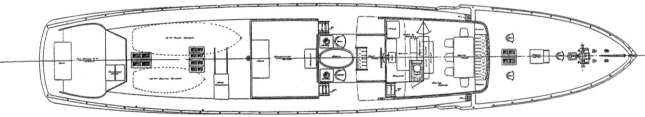

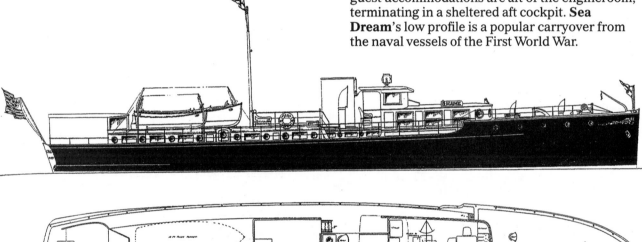

RAISED-DECK POWER CRUISER
1929 BY TAMS & KING

LOA	61′6″
Beam	14′0″
Draft	4′2″
Power	Two 60-hp Standard diesels
Source	January 1929, p. 61

Carved scrollwork and hawsepipes adorn the bow and help offset the too-numerous portholes that march along the raised-deck portion of the hull. The long, sweeping transition to the main deck however, is very attractive. Below deck, accommodations have been sacrificed in favor of plenty of storage space and a good-sized engineroom. Instead of placing the ’midships toilet room to

starboard (right where the owner and his party will be boarding), that part of the interior layout might have been better as a mirror image of what’s shown; this would have the additional benefit of placing direct access to the main cabin to starboard where it’s most needed. In all, in spite of the minor criticisms above, this is a well-proportioned, stately, and inspiring design.

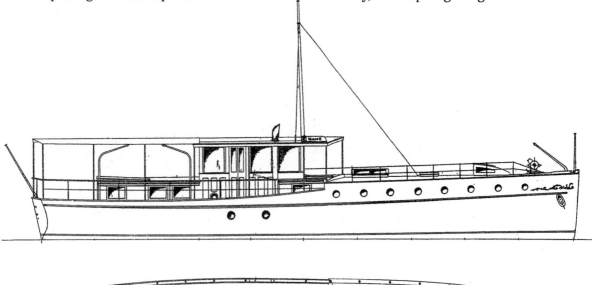

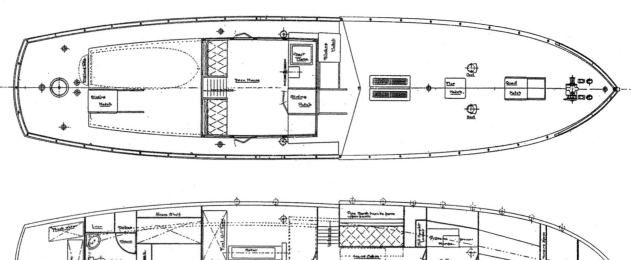

POWER CRUISER OF 1927
BY LEE & BRINTON

LOA	64'0"
Beam	13'10"
Draft	4'0"
Power	Two 225-hp Sterling Dolphin gasoline engines
Source	September 1927, p. 64

Early California informal style is apparent here in the wraparound settees, the two double berths, and the pair of staterooms that, by use of a sliding panel, can become one. The helmsman, more often than not a paid professional, occupies the same deckhouse as the owner and his party—whereas on the East Coast he'd more apt to be in a separate, often unsheltered, location. Madden & Lewis of Sausalito were the builders.

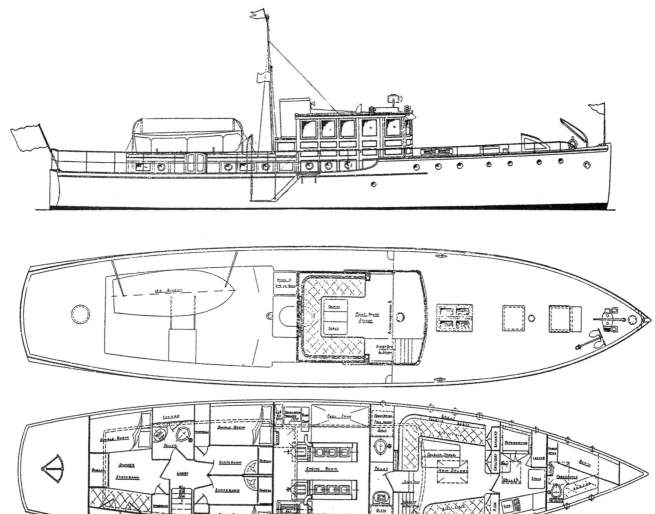

COMMUTER OF 1928 BY NEW YORK LAUNCH & ENGINE CO.

LOA	55′0″
Beam	10′0″
Power	Two 150-hp gasoline engines
Source	February 1928, p. 55

Because she's basically a day boat with no need for much in accommodations, low freeboard and inconspicuous cabins prevail to create an overall rakish profile. The extreme tumblehome at the transom helps as well. Although low, the cabins have plenty of window area to bring in natural light, with the trunk cabin fenestration done Luders-style. Strangely, there's no aft cockpit, so the settee by the steering wheel is where the on-deck comfort is to be found.

POWER CRUISER OF 1927
BY DAWN BOAT CORP.

LOA	45'0"
Beam	11'0"
Draft	3'6"
Power	Two 65-hp Kermath gasoline engines
Source	May 1927, p. 61

There's a lot of living space crammed into this yacht: two double staterooms, three toilets, a galley, and crew's quarters way forward. So it was with standardized cruisers, created for a wide appeal among yachtsmen who chose to economize. Compared to rival production builders such as Elco, Dawn built fewer offerings with lower profiles. In 1927, for example, Dawn had only one other (smaller) model available.

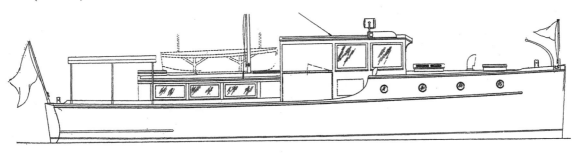

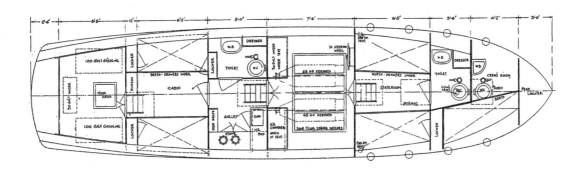

POWER CRUISER OF 1927
BY GEO. F. LAWLEY & SON CORP.

LOA	60′0″
LWL	59′2″
Beam	14′0″
Draft	3′6″
Power	Two 6-cylinder Sterling Chevron gasoline engines
Source	March 1927, p. 95

What a glorious deckhouse! It's a bit high because it rests on the deck instead of being a step-down affair like the previous designs of this chapter. Angling the forward corners, a contemporary technique for yachts of this type, helps eliminate an otherwise boxy appearance. Gasoline engines were common in the 1920s since diesels had yet to come into their own, and as a means of protection against an engineroom fire or explosion, steel bulkheads are called for. In order to get the desired accommodations aft of the engineroom bulkhead, the berths and bureau of the owner's stateroom extend a little under the aft deck and, along with the water tanks, preclude an aft cockpit. So if you want open-air seating, you go to the cushioned skylight that adjoins the deckhouse on its forward face. Stately, rather than sleek, best describes this yacht.

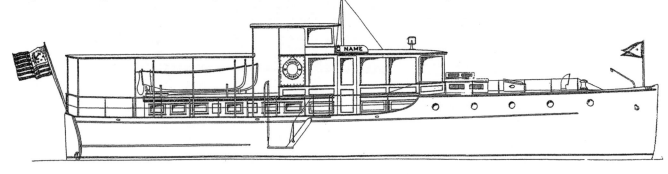

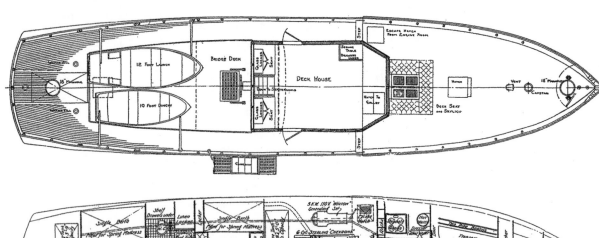

POWER CRUISER JANETELL OF 1928 BY WILLIAM J. DEED

LOA	53'0"
Beam	12'0"
Draft	3'11"
Power	60-hp Standard diesel
Source	June 1928, pp. 44-45

Family cruisers, as we know them today, were rare in the years before the Great Depression when yachts were commonly manned by a paid crew. But **Janetell** is an exception. Her design differs as well in that the published drawings are so numerous and so detailed. Thanks to the sectional views, one has little doubt as to how each compartment looked. (The brick-like bulkhead treatment took a while to understand, though, until I realized that this is a view of the tiled shower stall.) I count berthing for 11 persons—many more than the average cruiser of **Janetell**'s size. It's a fine design in all respects, but of quite a different character from Deed's later work. His legacy consists of the boxy sheet-plywood boats that followed **Janetell**, the drawings for which are at Mystic Seaport.

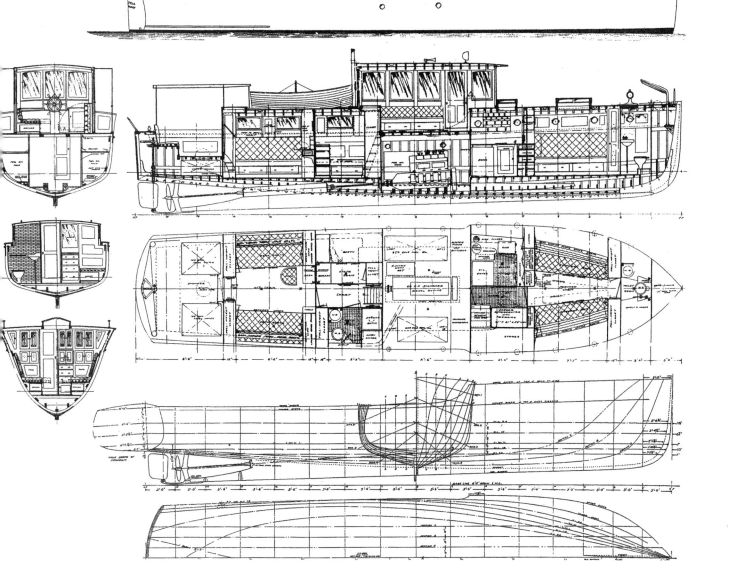

COMMUTER OF 1931 BY ELDREDGE-McINNIS

LOA	40′6″
Beam	10′11″
Draft	3′0″
Power	Two 180-hp Sterling Petrel gasoline engines
Source	December 1931, p. 54

Selected from at least three similar designs because of the reproducibility of its drawings, this and baby commuters in general make ideal cruisers. The larger **Marlin**—same type, same designer—owned for many years by the Kennedy family is best known, perhaps, but the standardized 38-footers turned out by Chris-Craft are still popular as well. The boat shown here features a forward cockpit large enough for four rattan chairs—the mark of a true yacht—and the versatile cabin aft of it converts for sleeping a party of four. Originally, the tiny aft cabin was intended for a paid hand, but today would find more appropriate use, say, in giving a couple of small children a taste of independent living.

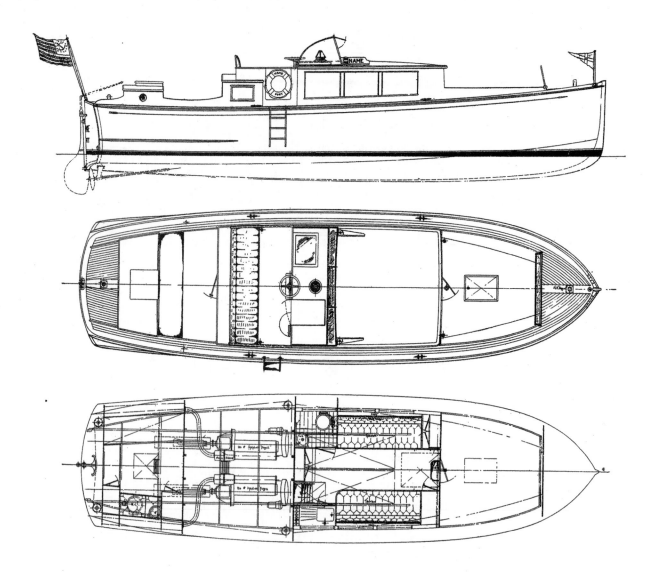

COMMUTER OF 1930
BY JOHN L. HACKER

LOA	38'0"
Beam	8'5"
Draft	2'3"
Power	Two 200-hp Kermath gasoline engines
Source	February 1930, p. 74

Though this boat was designed more for smooth-water speed and less for cruising than the previous design, there's still a place to cook and sleep within the streamlined cabin. Because designer John Hacker lived near the Detroit auto makers, he, like them, ranked stylishness high in his list of design parameters. Not surprisingly, Hacker's boats featured auto-like elements, as in the wind-shield and cabin treatment shown here. And this commuter is as slippery and fast as it looks, with a speed of 42 miles an hour.

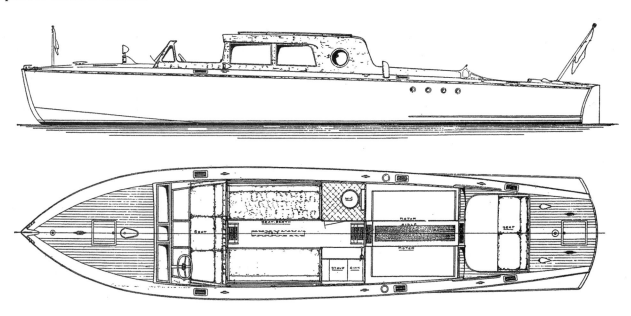

COMMUTER **MISS LARCHMONT IV**
OF 1931 BY PURDY BOAT CO.

LOA	40'0"
LWL	39'4"
Beam	10'3"
Draft	2'5"
Power	Two 6-cylinder Scripps gasoline engines
Source	August 1931, p. 55

My first exposure to what commuting by water was all about came through this Purdy-built yacht, whose owner at the time summered on the island of Islesboro in Penobscot Bay, Maine. She'd been renamed **Nana**, and you recognized her by the size of her bow wave, through which you could occasionally get a glimpse of her lovely Bermuda-green hull. Maintained to perfection, she soon became this grade-schooler's favorite among all the island yachts that arrived and departed from my home town of Rockland. You could hear her at great distance, just as you could the other fast, high-powered craft, so it's not surprising that as engines became noisier, forward cockpits gained popularity. You could even steer from this one!

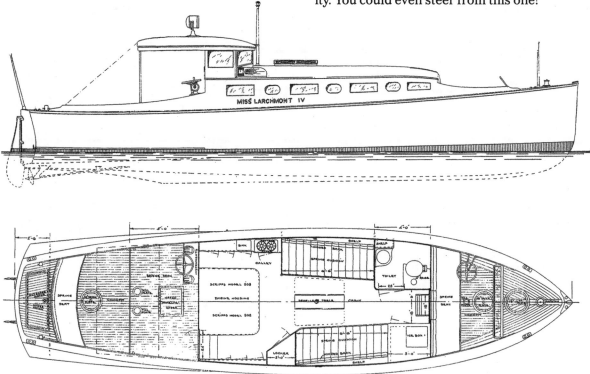

CRUISETTE OF 1935 BY ELCO

LOA	38′ 5″
Beam	10′ 6″
Draft	3′ 7″
Power	Elco-Buda gasoline engines of various sizes
Source	April 1935, p. 50

"Cruisette" became the model designation for the smaller creations built and offered by Elco as standardized power cruisers. This one was known as the Elco Cruisette 38, and was one of several 1935 offerings in a sales approach duplicating that of automobile manufacturers. Streamlining took the 1930s by storm and appeared in boats like this as well as in autos, airplanes, toasters, and most other aspects of American life during the Great Depression. Windshields and cabin fronts that slant back, as well as roof lines with compound curves have been adopted here as relatively mild concessions to the streamlined age. Boats of this type with an extended pilothouse that could be closed to the weather soon took on the name "sedan cruiser" for obvious reasons.

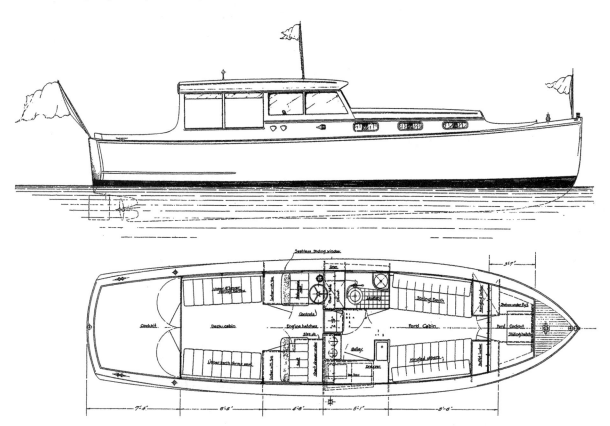

POWER CRUISER NATALON II
OF 1933 BY ELCO

LOA	60′0″
Beam	13′10″
Draft	3′6″
Power	Two 6-cylinder 145-hp Elco gasoline engines
Source	March 1933, p. 54

This is a customized power cruiser that's quite like a so-called Elco "flat top," but with the pilothouse raised for better visibility and a larger deckhouse. It's interesting that the drawing shows only a combined bureau and desk as built-in furniture—treating the space just as a land-based architect might depict a living room. The space is living room sized as well, measuring a virtually unobstructed 10′ by 11½′. **Natalon**'s stately profile carries over from the previous decade, the rake of her windshields being the only nod to the streamlined age.

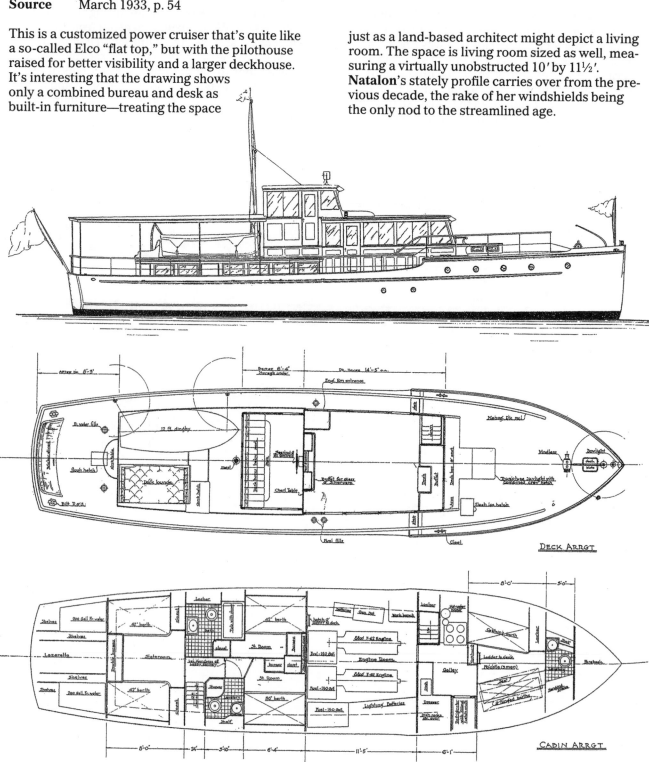

DECK ARRGT

CABIN ARRGT

COMMUTER OF 1930
BY CONSOLIDATED
SHIPBUILDING CORP.

LOA   62'0"
Beam   11'6"
Power   Two 300-hp Speedway gasoline engines
Source   January 1930, p. 65

Because her bridge is open and her profile low,
this boat looks fast. She is. With all 600 horsepower cranked up, she'd do 27 miles an hour.
Commuter owners often took their breakfast
while they raced down the East or Hudson rivers on
the way to work, so their boats were fitted with a
minimal galley. Depending upon the weather
and his personal preference, the owner of this
yacht could enjoy the open air from either
the forward or aft cockpit.

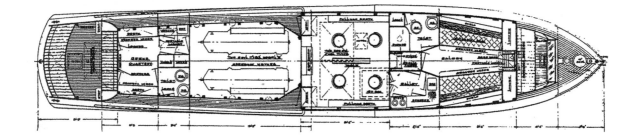

DIESEL COMMUTER OF 1935
BY JOHN H. WELLS

LOA	67'0"
LWL	65'5"
Beam	12'7"
Draft	3'6"
Power	Two 180-hp gasoline or diesel engines
Source	December 1935, pp. 42-43

Weighing half again more than an equivalent gasoline engine and costing over twice as much, it's easy to understand why diesel engines were slow to catch on—despite their being much safer than gas engines. This yacht was designed to accept either, although it's clear from the drawings that diesel was preferred. And at 20 miles an hour, she'd be only 1 mile an hour slower, but ever so much safer. Like the 1935 Elco shown earlier, the raking windshield is all that has given way to streamlining. Although called a commuter by her designer, this yacht is laid out more for cruising, with two double staterooms sharing an adjacent bathtub-equipped toilet room.

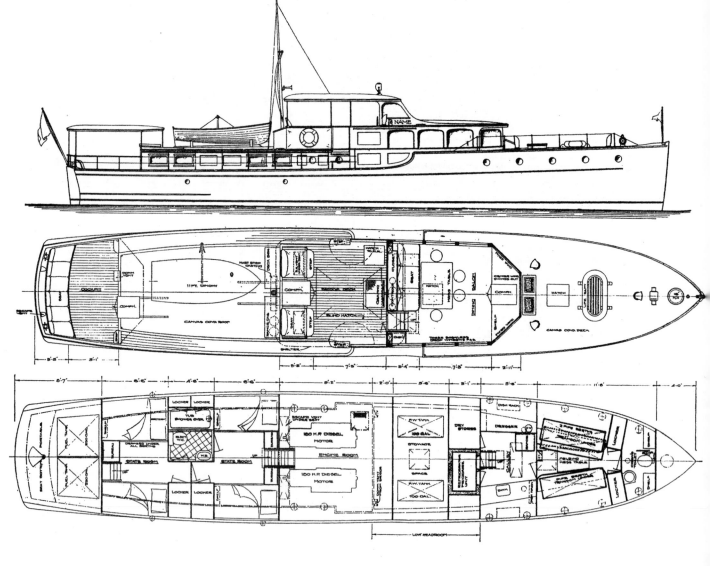

POWER CRUISER **HIPPOCAMPUS**
OF 1931 BY A. E. LUDERS, SR.

LOA	75'0"
LWL	74'0"
Beam	16'0"
Draft	4'9"
Power	Two 200-hp Sterling gasoline engines
Source	January 1931, p. 66

Besides the familiar alternating round and rectangular window treatment, Luders frequently utilized an ogee transition between the raised and main decks. He also favored half elliptical shapes for the tops of large deckhouse windows. No matter whether she was a 40-footer or a major cruising yacht like this, A. E. Luders's ability to blend his favorite design elements into a pleasing overall effect was legendary—and distinctive, as well. **Hippocampus**, built at her designer's Stamford, Connecticut, yard for James F. Porter, was homeported at Great Spruce Head Island in Penobscot Bay and appeared regularly in Maine coast waters during the 1930s.

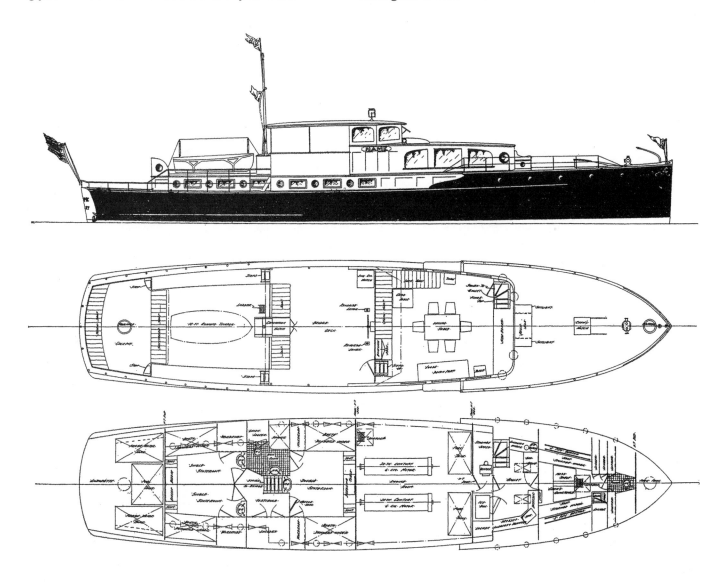

MOTOR YACHT **CUTTY SARK**
OF 1932 BY ELDREDGE-McINNIS

LOA	90′6″
LWL	89′10″
Bearn	16′11″
Draft	4′8″
Power	Two 200-hp Winton diesels
Source	February 1933, p. 53

Walter McInnis (the partner who did the designing) could be counted upon when it came to drawing good-looking vessels of any type, but his large power craft are always noteworthy. His treatment of **Cutty Sark**'s raised foredeck and its extension cuts down on her apparent freeboard as well as allowing real windows to be used instead of portholes. **Cutty Sark** was built in Neponset, Massachusetts, by Geo. F. Lawley & Son, and her designer's collection of drawings up to 1950 have been donated to Mystic Seaport.

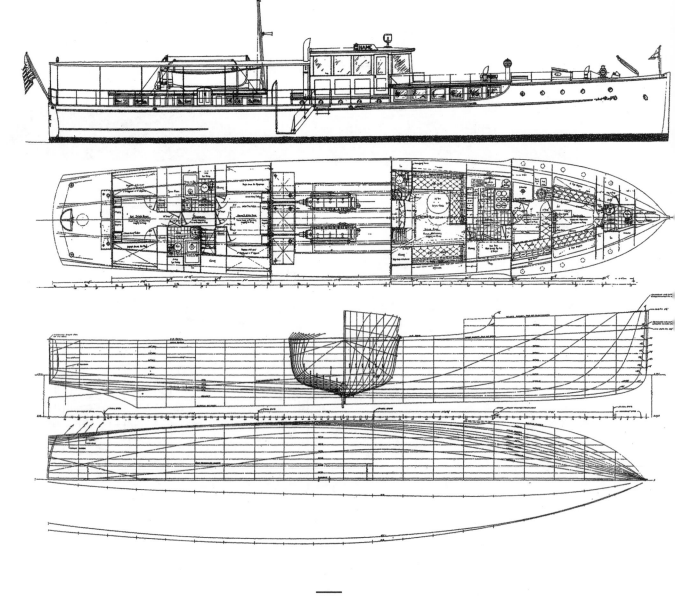

POWER CRUISER OF 1932
BY HENRY C. GREBE

LOA	65'0"
Beam	13'0"
Draft	3'6"
Power	Two 500-hp Winton gasoline engines
Source	February 1932, p. 72

Just as in the naval destroyers that inspired this and the many other similar designs, a key performance parameter was dryness in rough weather—that is, to take as little spray aboard as possible. A raised foredeck accomplished this in both vessel types, and resulted in an aesthetically pleasing profile to boot. Most of the fast and racy power cruisers originated on the East Coast where the majority of the country's design offices were located. Henry Grebe's Chicago address made him an exception, and his many fine designs prove that his eye for form and proportion were as good as or better than that of his contemporaries.

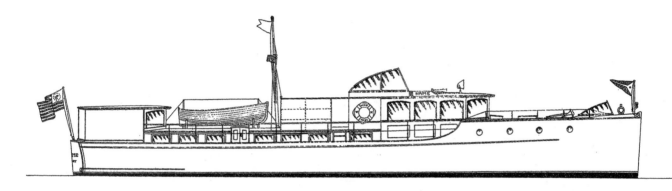

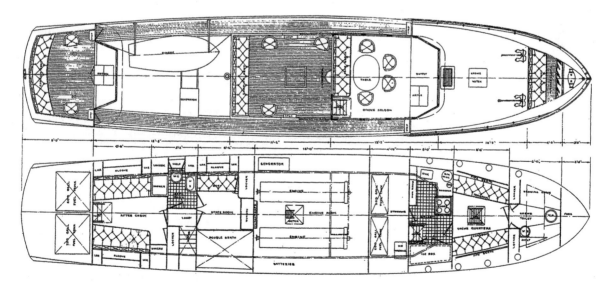

POWER CRUISER OF 1935
BY MASTERSON & SCHLEGEL

LOA	55'0"
Beam	18'6"
Source	October 1935, p. 42

The Great Depression left design offices with far less commissioned work than they enjoyed during the heady days of the previous decade, so designers turned to speculative creations, hoping to attract a client or two. The ability to operate economically widened the appeal of any new yacht, and showed up more and more often in the write-ups that accompanied any published design. Slower boats and efficient engines helped keep running costs down—a single, moderate-sized diesel and a speed of 12 miles an hour were mentioned for this one, for example. Superb drafting was another result of designers having time on their hands. In this regard, Masterson & Schlegel turned out masterpieces.

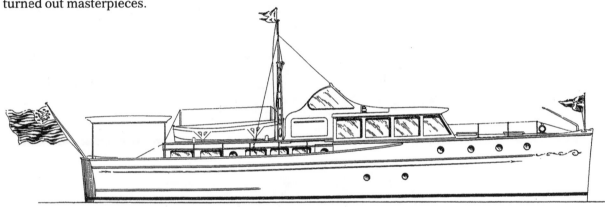

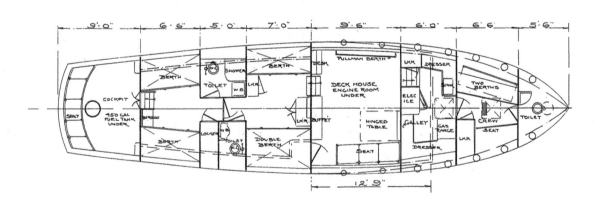

POWER CRUISER OF 1934
BY ALBERT MEHL

LOA	68'0"
Beam	14'0"
Draft	3'6"
Power	Two 100-hp diesels
Source	May 1934, p. 40

Few, including me, are familiar with this New York designer's work, but mighty good work it is. Mehl's style of emphasizing bedding upholstery, and cabin sole patterns makes his plan views easier than most to understand. The layout is pretty conventional for the type and era, but the stately profile looks more mid-1920s than mid-'30s. Despite her outward appearance, the diesel power and moderate speed of 15 miles an hour reflect the economic reality of the times. Accommodations remain about the same as earlier, however. The main saloon's dining table can easily seat ten. That space also contains a 1930s entertainment center in its forward, starboard corner— consisting of a Victrola and radio.

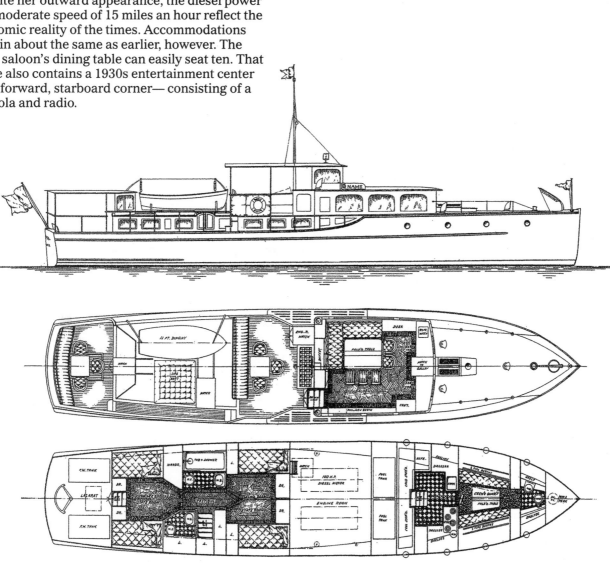

SPORTFISHING CRUISER
HILLHARRE OF 1935
BY A. M. DEERING

LOA	40'0"
LWL	39'6"
Beam	10'6"
Draft	3'0"
Power	8-cylinder Gray 340 gasoline engine
Source	March 1935, p. 58

Moderately streamlined with an automobile-inspired pilothouse, **Hillharre** still looks attractive even after 65 years. Deering's handling of the transition between the trunk cabin and pilothouse, which incorporates a continuous belt line under the windows and a faired-in lower windshield edge, are both distinctive and handsome. Judging from the plan view, her hull had great flare forward and extreme tumblehome aft, making her a worthy progenitor of the shapely Florida sportfishermen. **Hillharre**'s builder was J. Walter Jones of Wittman, Maryland.

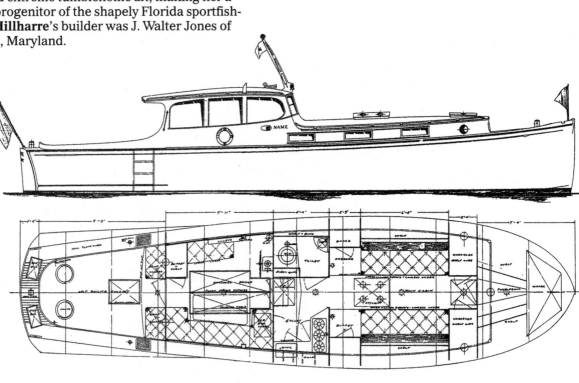

EXPRESS CRUISER
OF 1935 BY A.C.F.

LOA	47′0″
Beam	11′0″
Power	Two Hall-Scott Invader gasoline engines
Source	February 1935, p. 66

The name express cruiser was once used to describe power cruisers having bridge decks and windshields, instead of pilot houses, like this one. The implication was speed. This boat, for example, was expected to do 30 mph. She's essentially a day boat with lots of cockpit space, both forward and aft. She'd be fine for cruising as well, as long as one is content with the basics. The dinette converts to a berth on the port side, while opposite, by swinging up the starboard backrest, an upper and lower berth are created. The drawings are by A. W. W. vanHoorn, who at the time was staff naval architect for A. C. F. (American Car and Foundry, in full name). He had a good eye and succeeded in blending several contemporary elements, none of which are overdone, into a nice looking overall profile.

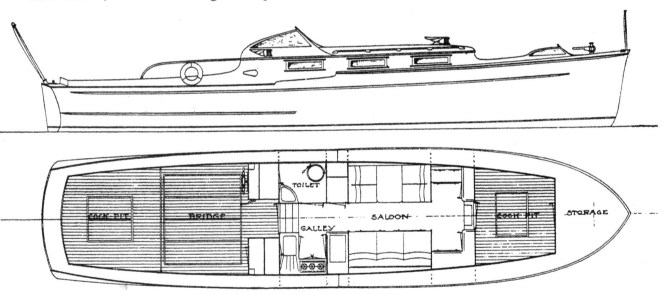

POWERBOATS

COMMERCIAL MILITARY & MISCELLANEOUS CRAFT

STEAM TUG **OX** OF 1907
BY BURGESS & PACKARD

LOA	38′0″
LWL	36′0″
Beam	10′4″
Draft	5′0″
Power	30-hp steam engine
Source	August 1907, p. 677

Because of this tug's small size, a single licensed engineer could legally operate **Ox**, whose mission was to service the Marblehead, Massachusetts, boatyard of her designer/builder. Coal served as fuel, and the cost of operation was claimed to be about half that of an equivalent gasoline engine. The trial trip's speed was 9.9 miles an hour. **Ox** operated in the near silence characteristic of steam engines.

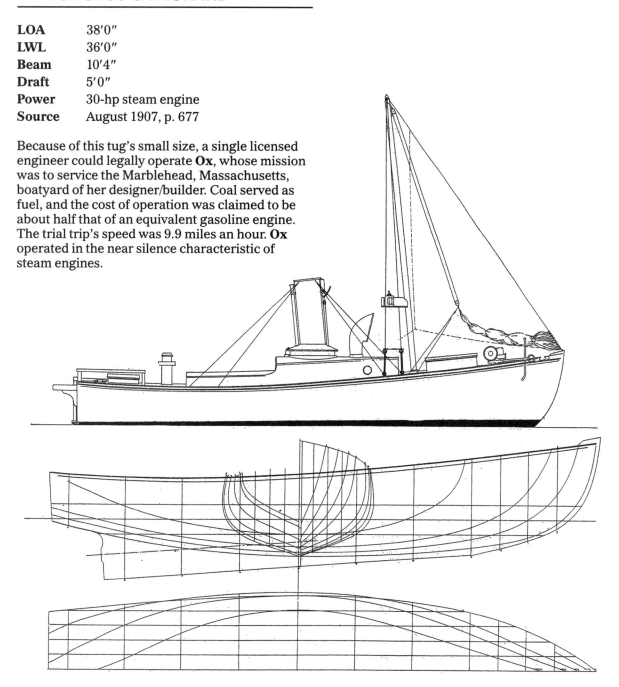

DIESEL TUG OF 1926
BY BROWN & DEMAREST

LOA	50'0"
Beam	13'6"
Draft	6'5"
Power	150-hp Bessemer diesel
Source	December 1926, pp. 50-51

The drawings for this cute little harbor tug contain lots of detail on how traditional cabins and deckhouses are supposed to look—detail that can be applied to other types of workboat-inspired designs even now. Visor, windows, cabintop edge moldings, smokestack, nameboards, and running lights, for example, show clearly. Construction features show as well. Purpose built, the power plant consumes the space below deck as well as all of the lower cabin aft of the pilothouse. This is a dayboat for use around the New York waterfront, without many accommodations, built sufficiently rugged to survive being knocked around as she executes her intended mission.

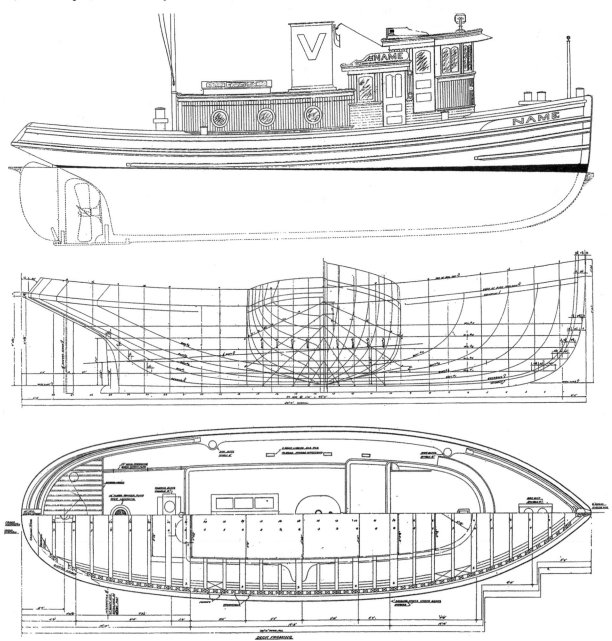

DIESEL TUGBOAT **CRAIG** OF 1924 BY J. MURRAY WATTS

LOA	64'6"
Beam	14'10"
Draft	7'0"
Power	150-hp Fairbanks-Morse diesel
Source	March 1924, p. 46

Craig Brothers Marine Railway Co. built this harbor tug for its own use in waters around Norfolk, Virginia, at the south end of Chesapeake Bay. She's unusually handsome and represents a style that survived for half a century. When the word "tugboat" is mentioned, this profile is what invariably comes to mind.

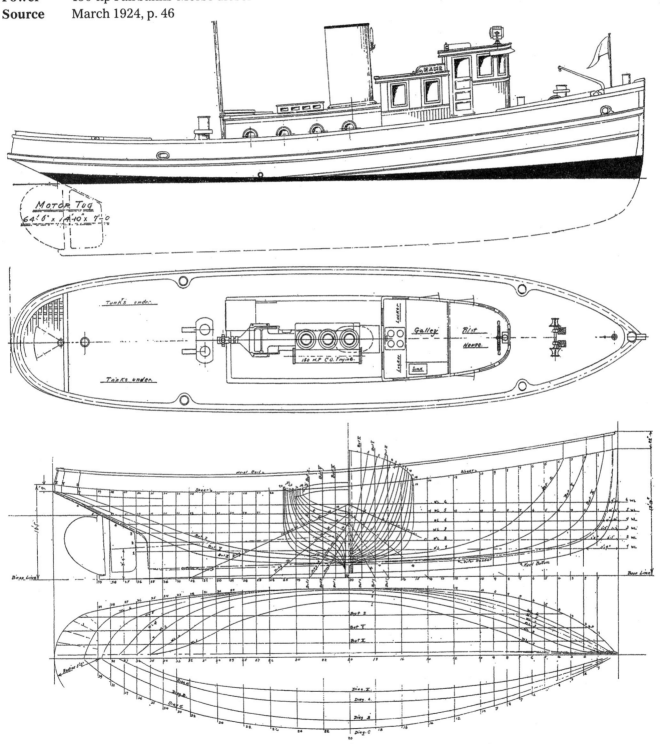

U.S. ARMY UTILITY BOAT OF 1909
BY DEPARTMENT OF THE ARMY

LOA	60′0″
Beam	12′0″
Draft	4′0″
Displ.	25 tons
Power	100-hp 4-cylinder Craig gasoline engines
Source	January 1909, pp. 42-43

A contract for four boats of this design was awarded to The Matthews Boat Co. of Port Clinton, Ohio, along with 60 pages of written specifications that had to be complied with. Looking more like a graceful, turn-of-the-century glass cabin launch, with its half-elliptical windows, than anything designed by the Army, only the finest materials were permitted, which meant, among other things, that all of the fastenings were non-ferrous. Carrying troops and towing targets for gunnery practice were among their duties, so seating is abundant and there's a towing bitt on the aft deck.

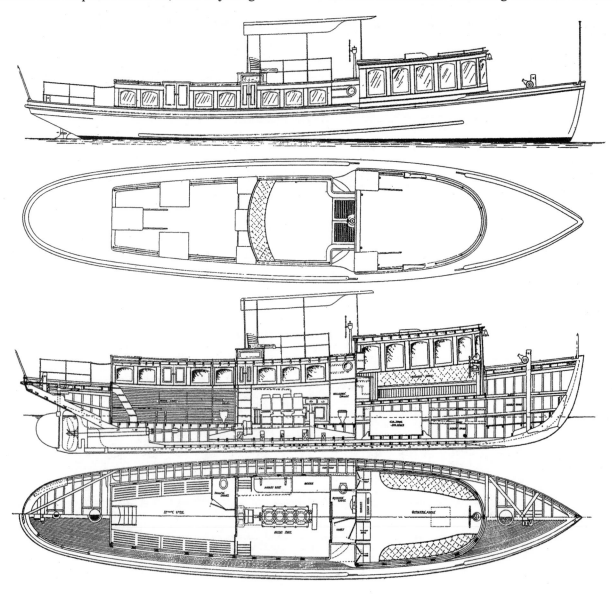

U.S. NAVAL PATROL BOAT OF 1916 BY A. E. LUDERS

LOA	66′0″
Beam	13′3″
Draft	4′6″
Power	Two 400-hp 12-cylinder Van Blerck gasoline engines
Source	August 1916, pp. 370-71

Eighteen hundred gallons of fuel gave this craft a 500-mile range at 25 miles an hour; top speed was 30. Although this one was built under a government contract by Luders Marine Construction Co. of Stamford, Connecticut, as a sample boat, many subsequent patrol craft were privately built to a variety of designs, to be used as yachts but available for patriotic duty on short notice. Most looked like baby destroyers, with serious-looking plumb stems and transom stems like this one. Besides lots of tankage for fuel, they mounted a gun or two.

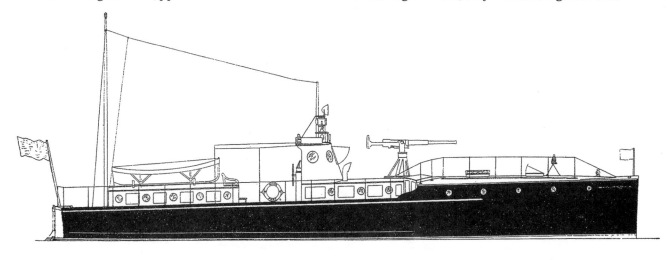

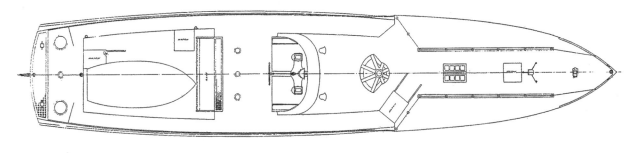

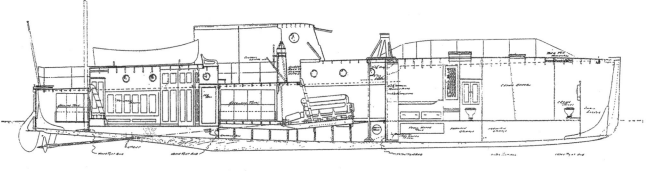

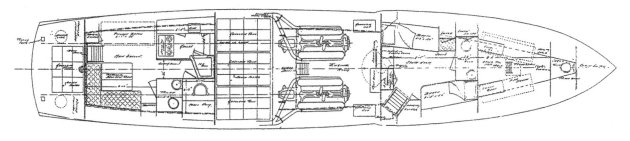

POLICE BOAT OF 1937
BY ELDREDGE-McINNIS

LOA	38′3″
Beam	10′5″
Draft	3′0″
Power	270-hp Hall-Scott Invader gasoline engine
Source	June 1937, p. 37

When picket boats were needed for coastal patrol during the Second World War, this design, prepared for the Boston Police Department, was the one selected. Contracts were let to small yards throughout the country, and many 38′ picket boats poured forth. They were among the best-looking of the many boats of the war years, and afterwards found use as pleasure craft as well as training boats for the Sea Scouts.

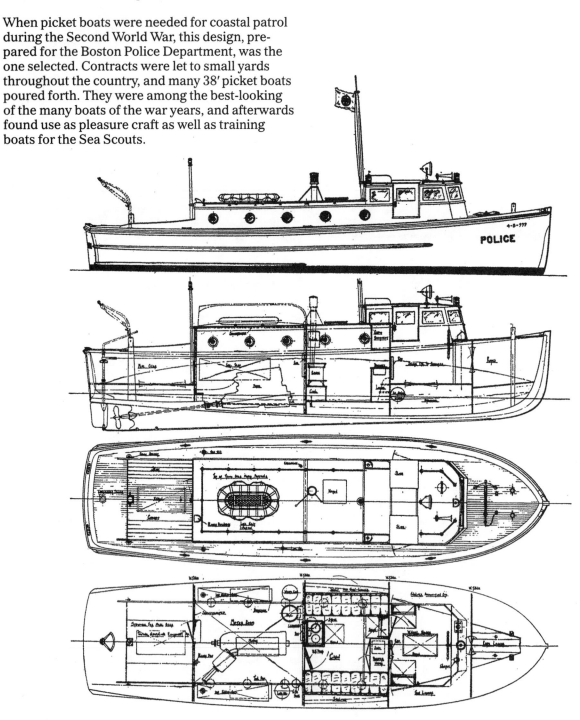

MISSION VESSEL **SUNBEAM**
OF 1939 BY TAMS, INC.

LOA	72′ 0″
LWL	67′ 7″
Beam	17′ 6″
Draft	6′ 0″
Power	230-hp Superior diesel
Source	July 1939, p. 40

Sunbeam was built in Damariscotta, Maine, by Harry Marr for the Maine Coast Missionary Society, and was the third boat of the same name whose work was to help spread the word of God among Maine's isolated island communities. The word "saloon" somehow flies in the face of "God's Tugboat" as **Sunbeam** was affectionately nick- named. Yet you'll notice that she has not one saloon, but two. If an island were without a church, worship took place in **Sunbeam**'s deck saloon, followed, perhaps, by a welcome meal in the dining saloon below deck. Al Mason designed **Sunbeam** under Tams's letterhead, and followed the longstanding practice in naming onboard gathering spaces saloons. (These days, "saloon" has become "salon" among the more genteel, despite tradition.) As **Sunbeam** sometimes had to thrash her way to the Maine island communities in harsh winter weather, a high bow, cutaway fore- foot, and greenheart ice sheathing were called for. Painted gray with white deckhouses, **Sunbeam** looked as handsome and businesslike in the flesh as she does here in print.

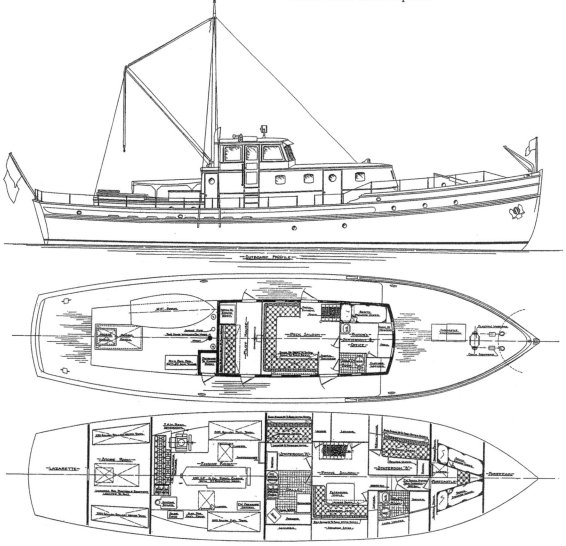

WORKBOAT **MANATEE** OF 1921
BY J. C. KIMMETH

LOA	37'9"
LWL	34'2"
Beam	10'2"
Draft	4'0"
Power	40-hp Frisbie gasoline engine
Source	June 1921, pp. 21-24

What convinced *The Rudder* to feature a purpose-designed workboat as a how-to-build remains a mystery, as does the designer himself. But for anyone who desires a rugged and shapely, low-speed, engine-driven hull for any purpose, these plans could serve as a guide. Even the accompanying text indicated several adaptations using this one hull design: general cargo work, commercial fishing, party fishing, and pleasure (possibly as a houseboat). The text is brief and without the usual instructions, but there are written specifications that describe each of the major timber elements such as keel, planking, and deckbeams. **Manatee** would look appropriate with commercial-grade construction, and offers endless possibilities.

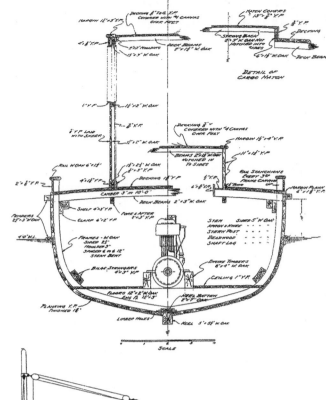

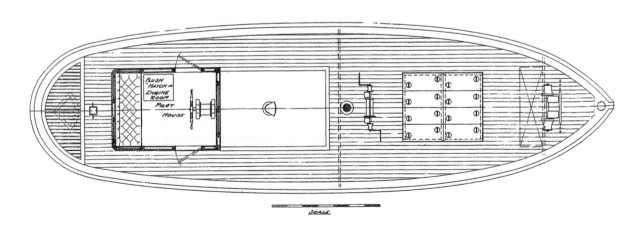

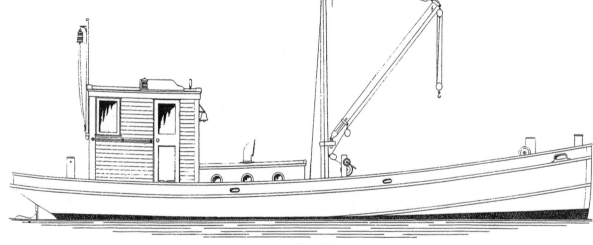

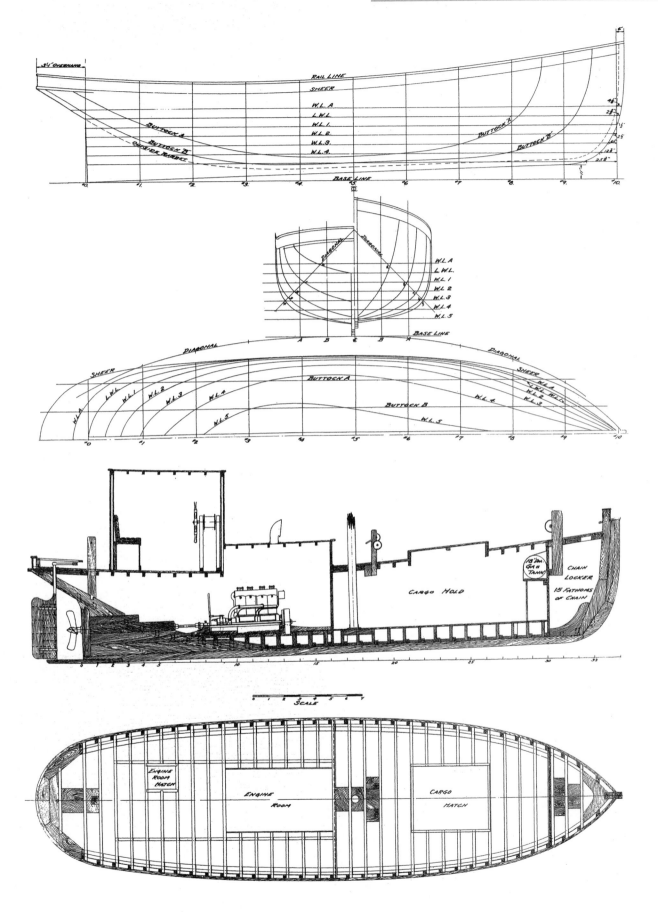

STEAM LIGHTER **MANZANILLO** OF 1906 BY SADLER, PERKINS & FIELD

LOA	100′0″
Beam	28′0″
Power	Sullivan 15 × 30″ compound steam engine
Source	April 1906, p. 272

Precious little text accompanied **Manzanillo**'s drawings, and there is no information at all on her construction details. The benefit of republishing the profile and deck plans here is simply to illustrate the general proportions of a vessel with a high and substantial deckhouse. It demonstrates how a design embodying attention to window style and arrangement, roof lines that sweep gracefully with the vessel's sheer, a rounded off and visored pilot-house, and a tall stack that rakes with the mast can really be attractive. After launching, **Manzanillo** went to Cuba where she was to be worked as a lighter shuttling cargoes between deep water freighters and the shore on weekdays, and as an excursion vessel on Saturdays and Sundays—thus the upper deck's slatted bench seats. **Manzanillo** was built on Staten Island, New York, by Roder-mond Bros. for Messrs. Owens & Co.

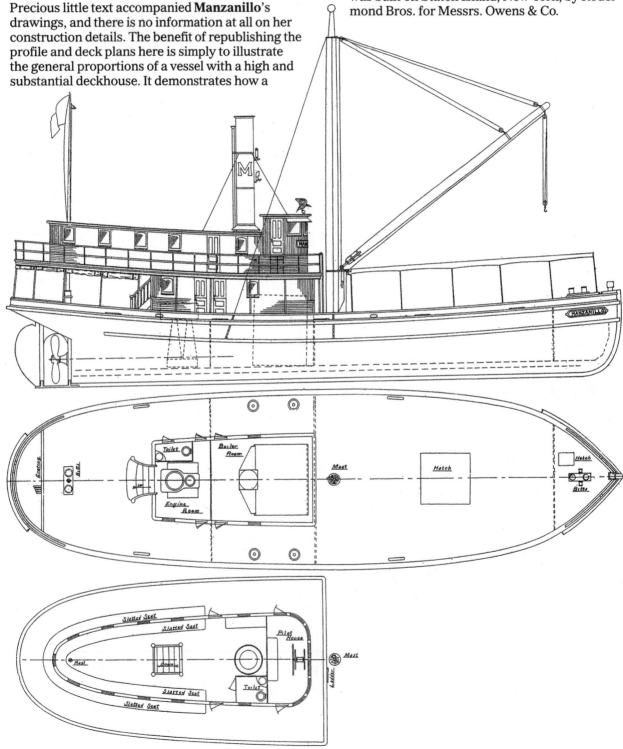

CARGO AND PASSENGER VESSEL **ROMA** OF 1928 BY J. MURRAY WATTS

LOA	70′0″
Beam	15′0″
Draft	4′6″ (7′0″ with cargo)
Power	Two 60-hp Fairbanks-Morse diesels
Source	February 1928, p. 58

Designer Watts created many designs, both pleasure and commercial, but he had a better eye for the latter than for the former, as **Roma** clearly indicates. Not only is this a fine-looking craft with correctly raking masts and stack but a practical one as well. Cargo can be distributed between the forward and after holds for the best trim, while passengers reside in staterooms, of which there are seven—four in the deckhouse, and three (including a double) below the main deck. Twin screws provide reliability as well as make the vessel more maneuverable at low speed. A configuration like this applied to, say, a sardine carrier, would make a dandy conversion. **Roma** was built by Bergoin & Bergoin for B. K. Thompson.

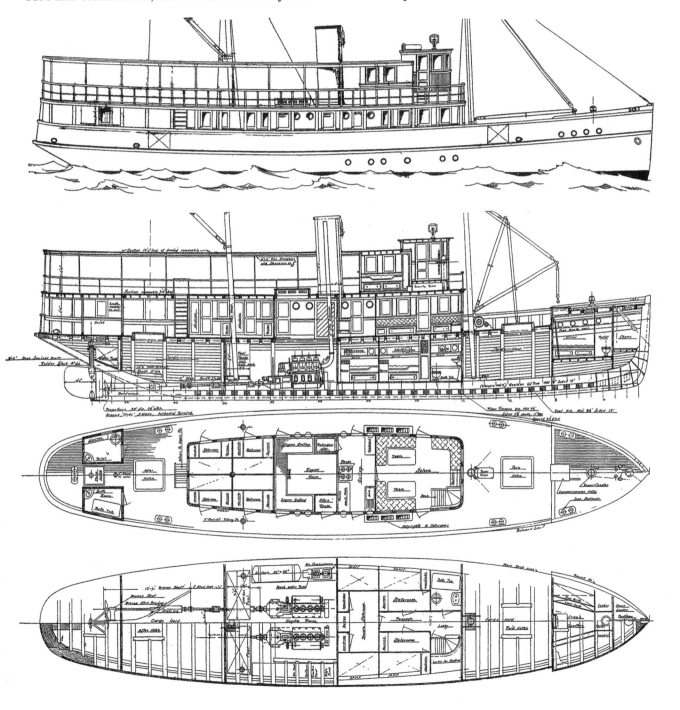

FISHING BOAT OF 1908
BY WILLIAM H. HAND, JR.

LOA	22'2"
LWL	21'7"
Beam	7'0"
Draft	1'10"
Power	Single-cylinder Lathrop gasoline engine
Source	December 1908, p. 340

Boats of this configuration once poured out of eastern Connecticut's boatshops and were used mostly for lobstering. Some had small, off-center pilothouses for steering in lieu of the sliding hatch shown here, and wet wells in which to store the day's catch were commonplace. Exactly why this particular fisherman went to the expense of commissioning a formal design remains a mystery, because the general practice was for a commercial builder to "model" the boats he built by means of a half model without benefit of formal drawings. In any event, here we have an idea of how these boats were shaped and built and, of course, modified by designer Hand to produce what he considered a suitable fishing boat. The result, if it looked as good as these drawings, would have been real sweet.

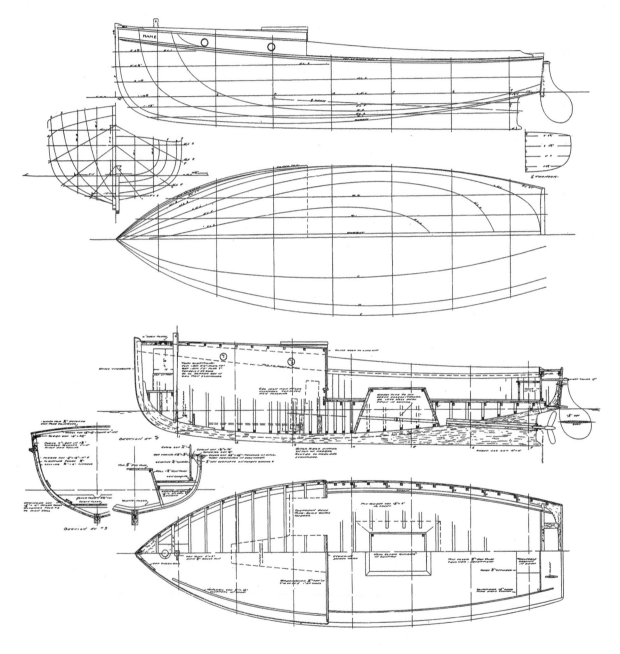

BUREAU OF FISHERIES SERVICE BOAT OF 1919 BY WILLIAM J. DEED

LOA	57'0"
Beam	12'9"
Draft	5'3"
Power	100-hp gasoline engine
Source	October 1919, pp. 479-81

More substantially built than a yacht, this hull even has arch-shaped hogging stringers for additional strength longitudinally. And despite the break in the deck, designer Deed has called for the main deck clamp and shelf to run all the way to the stem, which boosts the strength as well. Her unspecified main engine looks huge and was doubtless an easy-to-live-with, slow-turning, user-friendly beast. It exhausts through the starboard side of the hull rather than up a stack. Although not mentioned in the accompanying text, her big propeller looks as if it might be of the controllable-pitch type. There's a small wing engine that can be coupled to the main shaft in an emergency or when sustained very low speed is called for. A jib and mizzen can be set to dampen the vessel's roll in a beam sea, and the hoisting boom rigged from the mizzen mast handles the loads she is expected to carry from time to time. All in all, this is a rugged yet handsome design.

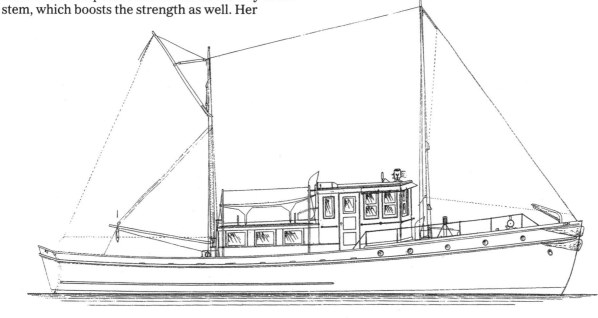

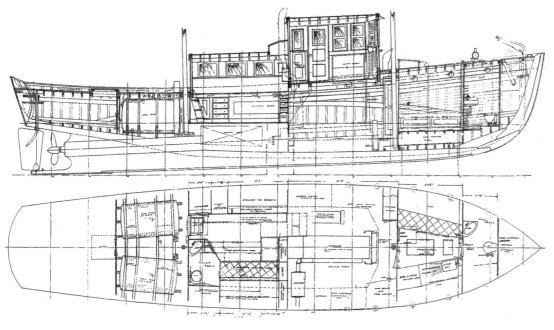

STEAM TRAWLER OF 1918
BY COX & STEVENS

LOA	150′0″
LWL	140′3″
Beam	25′0″
Draft	14′0″
Displ.	670 tons
Power	600-hp triple-expansion steam engine
Source	July 1918, pp. 337-40

Costing nearly four times as much as the Gloucester fishing schooners they were built to replace, and with a fish hold that was about that much more capacious, these big trawlers were not welcomed by sailormen or schooner owners. They harvested the sea more efficiently, for sure, and were still quite handsome to behold, having flaring bows aft of plumb stems, a graceful sheerline, a raking round stern, and deckhouses that complemented their overall appearance. They even set steadying sails. Indeed, in any other environment, these trawlers would have been very much appreciated. It was an era of change, however, and just as power was replacing sail, so steel was replacing wood as a construction material. And, finally, diesel replaced steam.

No matter—even though transitional, these trawlers from the Cox & Stevens office have some design fundamentals worth studying, whatever application you choose to put them to. There's the graceful sheer that sweeps up aft to balance the raised sheer forward. And there are the rakes and tapers of the masts and spars, with the matching rake of the smokestack. Overhanging cabintops with decorative edge moldings add only a little to the cost but much to the appearance. A pilothouse visor is always a nice touch and eliminates a "bald-headed" look, and a pilothouse front that's round or oval in plan view beats a flat-fronted one any day. While plain-faced plywood would serve as well

functionally for sides of a deckhouse, it's a relief to see vertical staving and raised panels in the doors.

Adopting eye-pleasing features often means increasing the cost of construction. But there's more to good living than an accountant's bottom line, and the pendulum may well have swung too far away from beauty and proportion during the second half of the 20th century in its quest for cost-effectiveness.

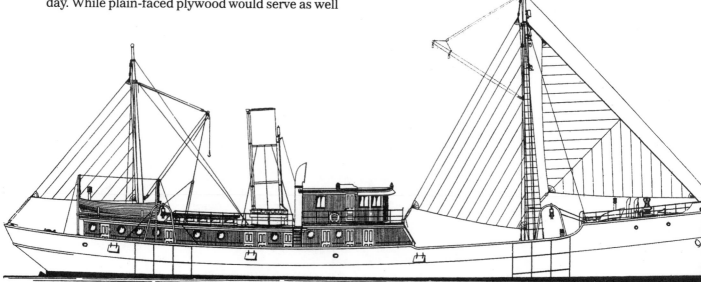

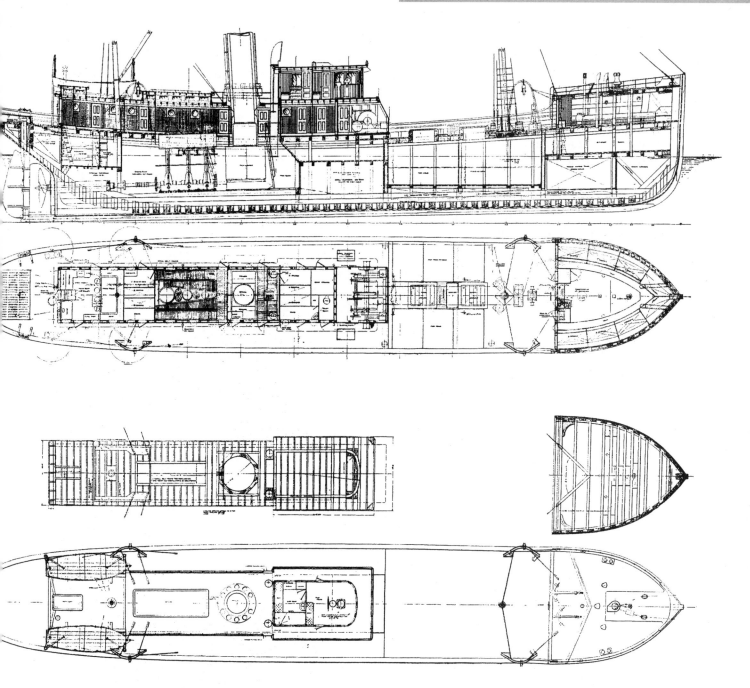

OYSTER BOAT **BLUEPOINTS**
OF 1937 BY FRANK H. ANDERSON

LOA	102′0″
Beam	28′0″
Draft	8′9″
Power	240-hp Fairbanks-Morse diesel
Source	June 1937, p. 36

Once wood was abandoned in favor of steel, beauty and grace diminished as well. Certainly no purpose-built steel oyster boat would look nearly as nice as **Bluepoints**, despite being perhaps more efficient. In any event, it was a treat to discover such a handsome working vessel within the pages of what is considered to be a magazine devoted to pleasure craft. Anderson & Coombes of New Haven, Connecticut, were the builders. In spite of this dredger's great length and beam, there's not much usable volume below deck, so the deckhouse contains the accommodations. Main deck support structure—beams, knees, stanchions, kingposts, etc.—takes much of what space there is, and serves the vital purpose of supporting the deck as it is heaped high with oysters each time they're dumped and culled from the dredges. It's heavy-duty work, but clearly this vessel is up to it.

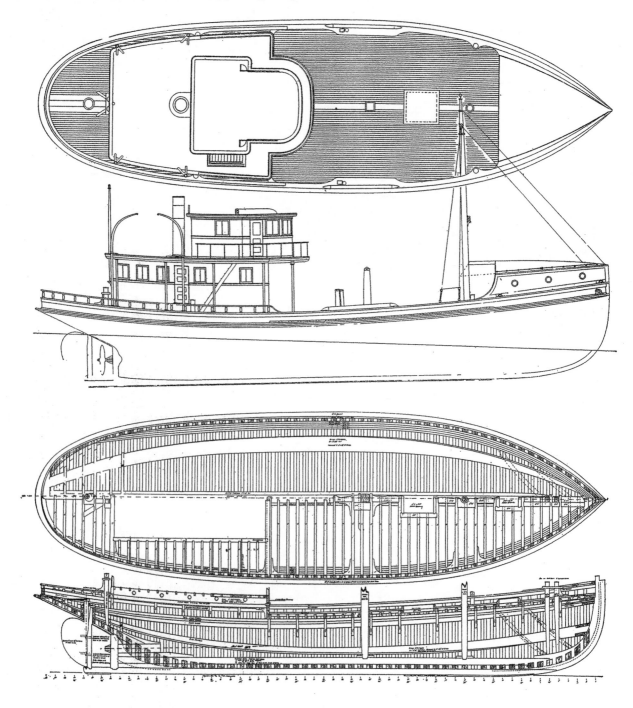

SELECTED DESIGNERS AND THEIR DRAWINGS

John G. Alden (1884–1962)
Prolific in a wide range of types and sizes, Alden made his name from the Malabar series of schooners. His office served as a training ground for Crocker, Peterson, Williams, Alberg, Nielsen, and others, and the firm is still in business today doing design and brokerage.

All drawings are at the Alden office: John G. Alden, Inc., 89 Commercial Wharf, Boston, MA 02110. The best source for further reading is the book *John G. Alden and His Yacht Designs*, by Carrick and Henderson, published by International Marine in 1983. *Yachting* featured an earlier, two-part article by William H. Taylor in its January and February 1962 issues.

Edwin A. Boardman (1886–1943)
Educated at Harvard, Boardman specialized in racing sailboats, especially the shallow-bodied, scow type favored by early measurement rules. He is best remembered as the designer of the Northeast Harbor A-class sloops.

Some drawings are at Hart Nautical Collections, MIT Museum, 265 Massachusetts Avenue, Cambridge, MA 02139. Boardman's book *Small Yachts*, published by Little, Brown and Co., 1920, is must reading for anyone interested in this designer.

W. Starling Burgess (1878–1947)
A talented and prolific designer of a wide range of types and sizes, both power and sail. Burgess associated with several partners over a career that began in the Boston area, relocated to New York, and wound up in Washington, D.C. He also designed aircraft in the years before the First World War. He is best remembered as the designer of the **America**'s Cup winners **Enterprise, Rainbow,** and the indomitable **Ranger** of 1937.

Many Burgess drawings are at Mystic Seaport, Greenmanville Avenue, Mystic, CT 06355 and at Hart Nautical Collections, MIT Museum, 265 Massachusetts Avenue, Cambridge, MA 02139. Several Burgess designs are featured in the book *Boat Plans at Mystic Seaport*, by Anne and Maynard Bray, published by Mystic Seaport in 2000.

The best source for further reading is a four-part article by Llewellyn Howland III in *Wooden-Boat* Nos. 71–74 (July 1986–February 1987). William H. Taylor also wrote about Burgess in the May 1947 issue of *Yachting*, and there's a revealing profile in the July 1937 *New Yorker*.

Concordia Co.
Specialized in wholesome cruising boats, with plans drawn by various designers working under the Concordia banner. Concordia yawls are the firm's best known design, of which 103 were built, mostly by the German firm of Abeking & Rasmussen.

Concordia drawings are at Mystic Seaport, Greenmanville Avenue, Mystic, CT 06355. (Drawings for the Concordia 31, first known as the Concordia 25, are available from The WoodenBoat Store, 1-800-273-7447.)

For the best in further reading, see Waldo Howland's two-volume *A Life in Boats*, published by Mystic Seaport in 1984 and 1988.

Consolidated Shipbuilding Corp.
One of the most prolific builders of launches, power cruisers, and motoryachts during the first half of the 20th century. Almost all were designed in-house. Located until mid-century at Morris Heights, New York, Consolidated began business as Gas Engine & Power Co., and Charles L. Seabury & Co. Seabury invented the naphtha engine, a compact device used in launches in lieu of steam plants in the days before gasoline engines.

Plans are at Mystic Seaport, Greenmanville Avenue, Mystic, CT 06355, which also has many photographs of Consolidated yachts and their launchings in its Rosenfeld Collection.

A definitive company history has yet to be written, but there is a good article in the February 1922 issue of *Motor Boating*.

Leigh H. Coolidge (1870–1959)
Coolidge moved west from the Boston area in 1890 where he had learned the shipwright's trade in local yards including Lawley's. Nicknamed "The Duke" because of his fancy dress and formal demeanor, Coolidge was a perfectionist who designed ferry-boats, tugboats, barges, and rumrunners, as well as yachts. The Miki tugs of World War II represent one of his best known designs.

The Seattle Museum of History and Industry, 2161 E. Hamlin Street, Seattle, WA 98102, holds Coolidge's plans.

For further reading, see the articles by Steve Bunnell in *Northwest Yachting* for April 1992.

Cox & Stevens
A prolific, New York–based design firm, in business from 1905 to 1946, with a wide-ranging output; designed very large yachts and commercial vessels, the latter work eventually taken over by Gibbs & Cox. The original partners of Cox & Stevens were the Cox Brothers, Daniel and Irving, and Col. Edwin A. Stevens. Philip L. Rhodes was the firm's designer from 1934 until 1947, when the business was renamed Philip L. Rhodes, Naval Architects.

Plans are at Mystic Seaport, Greenmanville Avenue, Mystic, CT 06355.

The best source for further reading is the book *Philip L. Rhodes and His Yacht Designs*, by Richard Henderson, published by International Marine in 1981.

S. S. Crocker (1890–1964)

An MIT graduate, Crocker worked early in his career at Alden's, then went into business for himself. His later designs were built by his son Sturgis in his Manchester, Massachusetts, boatyard. Crocker produced wholesome designs usually for cruising rather than racing—mostly sailboats below 50', along with some powerboats.

Plans are at the Peabody Essex Museum, East India Square, Salem, MA 01970.

The best source for further reading is *Sam Crocker's Boats: A Design Catalog*, by S. Sturgis Crocker, published by International Marine in 1985.

William F. Crosby (1891–1953)

A designer of easy-to-build boats for amateur construction, Crosby was editor of *The Rudder* and *Motor Boat* magazines, as well as author of several books including *Amateur Boat Building*, published by *The Rudder* in 1938. The Snipe-class sloops rank first as Crosby's best-known design, thousands having been built in all parts of the world.

To date, there has been no biography of Bill Crosby, although Boris Lauer-Leonardi, his successor at *The Rudder*, wrote an obituary that was published in the October 1953 issue. See also the seven-part series written by Crosby entitled "Forty Years of Yachting History," published in *The Rudder* from May to November 1930.

Some Crosby plans are at Mystic Seaport, Greenmanville Avenue, Mystic, CT 06355.

B. B. Crowninshield (1867–1948)

Crowninshield's designs were wide-ranging and many in number, and the drawings were consistently well drafted. A number of younger designers, including John G. Alden and William H. Hand, Jr., got their start working in the Crowninshield office. B. B. (for Bowdoin B.) established a big shipyard in Somerset, Massachusetts, about 1917 where he built wooden-hulled cargo schooners for World War I. He is best remembered for the seven-masted schooner **Thomas W. Lawson**, the **America**'s Cup candidate **Independence**, and the little and still-well-loved Dark Harbor 17½-footers.

Plans and other records are at the Peabody Essex Museum, East India Square, Salem, MA 01970.

Crowninshield's book *Fore and Afters*, published by Houghton Mifflin in 1940, is recommended reading, as are his annual catalogs, which feature several of his designs among the tide tables, brokerage listings, and other ephemera. This important designer deserves a more comprehensive treatment, but to date there has been no biography.

Thomas Fleming Day (1861–1927)

As the opinionated, original editor of *The Rudder*, Day contributed sufficiently to the **Sea Bird**'s design to claim credit as its co-designer. (Charles D. Mower actually drew the **Sea Bird**'s plans.) In this 27' yawl-rigged centerboarder, Day sailed across the Atlantic, then made the design famous by writing about it in his magazine. He repeated this promotional adventure with the double-ended powerboat **Detroit** a few years later. Never doubting a small boat's seagoing ability, he organized the first Bermuda Races, a major event long and subsequently sponsored by The Cruising Club of America.

You come to know Day best through his many writings in the early issues of *The Rudder*. He also wrote books such as *The Voyage of the Detroit, On Yachts and Yacht Handling, Hints to Young Yacht Skippers,* all published by *The Rudder. Across the Atlantic in Sea Bird,* published by Fore An' Aft Co. in 1927, is also a good read. *WoodenBoat* No. 43 (Nov./Dec. 1981) contains further information on Tom Day.

William J. Deed

A talented and versatile designer who at one time owned a boatyard in Nyack, New York. His career spanned the evolution of powerboats from their earliest days shortly after the turn of the century to the amateur-built plywood boats of the mid-1950s.

Deed's drawings of V-bottomed boats for sheet-plywood construction from the last half-dozen years of his career are at Mystic Seaport, Greenmanville Avenue, Mystic, CT 06355.

Motor Boating ran a number of Deed designs as how-to-build articles beginning in 1921. There is a brief mention of Deed's later life in Weston Farmer's book *From My Old Boat Shop,* published by International Marine in 1996.

W. Gilbert Dunham

An ingenious designer who, at various times, was in partnership under the name of Dunham & Stadel and Dunham & Timken. Dunham is best known for his **Stout Fella,** a small, standardized cruising sloop built by Mystic Shipyard in Mystic, Connecticut. His last design was the big, aluminum-hulled ketch **Firebird,** for his partner John Timken.

Some of Gil Dunham's drawings, including various versions of the **Stout Fella,** are at Mystic Seaport, Greenmanville Avenue, Mystic, CT 06355.

Elco

The designer and builder of standardized power cruisers called Cruisettes, located in Bayonne, New Jersey. Elco (for Electric Launch Co.) built 55 electric launches for the 1893 Chicago World's Fair and is said to have built some 6,000 pleasure boats. It was the 399 PT boats built for World War II that kept the Elco name going, but the plant was closed in 1949—a victim of its parent company, Electric Boat of Groton, Connecticut.

There is a comprehensive article in *Nautical Quarterly* No. 30 (Summer 1985) by William C. Swanson, and more information in Weston Farmer's book *From My Old Boat Shop,* published by International Marine in 1996. An Elco catalog of 1902 has been republished by Swanson Marine Enterprises in 1984.

Most of the Elco drawings burned in a 1963 fire, but a few are at Mystic Seaport, Greenmanville Avenue, Mystic, CT 06355 and The Mariners' Museum, 100 Museum Drive, Newport News, VA 23606.

Eldredge-McInnis

Walter McInnis (1893–1985) was the firm's designer, and an exceptionally talented one at that, who specialized in power craft. Before Eldredge-McInnis was founded in 1926, he had been with the Lawley yard in Neponset, Massachusetts, and the Nock yard in East Greenwich, Rhode Island. Besides yachts, McInnis designed a number of commercial powerboats as well as naval and Coast Guard craft.

Drawings through about 1950 are at Mystic Seaport, Greenmanville Avenue, Mystic, CT 06355. The remainder are with Alan McInnis (Walter's son), who carries on the Eldredge-McInnis name from his home (P.O. Box F, Hingham, MA 02043).

A fine, three-part article by Llewellyn Howland III was published in *WoodenBoat* Nos. 52, 53, and 54 (May–October 1983).

Martin C. Erismann (d. 1921)

Having studied naval architecture at Webb Academy (now Webb Institute) in this country and at the University of Glasgow in Scotland, Erismann designed steel ships as well as wooden pleasure craft. At one point he was associated with B. B. Crowninshield. His accidental death cut short what might have been an exceptional career in yacht design.

There is a brief piece on Martin Erismann in the July 1911 issue of *Motor Boating*. His replica Block Island boat **Roaring Bessie** was written up in Roger Taylor's *Good Boats*, published by International Marine in 1977.

Theodore E. Ferris (1872–1953)

New York–based designer of yachts, commercial, and military vessels who is most remembered for the cargo and troop ships of World War I. Ferris was associated with A. Cary Smith around the turn of the century, eventually becoming a partner. Later, during the war years, he became naval architect of the Emergency Fleet Corp. of the U.S. Shipping Board. It was in this capacity that he designed both wooden and steel vessels, built in large numbers on both coasts.

A comprehensive writeup on Ferris was published in the December 1917 issue of *The Rudder*.

William Gardner (1859–1934)

A graduate of Cornell University and The Royal Naval College in England, Gardner opened a New York design office in 1888 at No. 1 Broadway. He specialized in the design of sailing yachts for racing. The three-masted schooner-yacht **Atlantic,** which held the transatlantic sailing record of 12 days and 4 hours for almost a century, and the **America**'s Cup contender **Vanitie** are Gardner's most remembered designs. He designed to both the Universal and International measurement rules and his yachts took consistent honors. He also designed steam yachts and commercial vessels, all having an artistic quality with great eye appeal.

Tragically, Gardner's drawings seem not to have survived, with the exception of the few that have been published.

The best biography is by Gardner's associate Francis Sweisguth that appeared in the April 1951 issue of *Yachting*.

Henry J. Gielow (1855–1925)

Although he specialized in large vessels, commercial and pleasure, as well as their power plants, Gielow occasionally turned out smaller craft. He is best remembered for the lovely steam and diesel yachts such as **Delphine,** the 258-footer for Mrs. Horace Dodge.

Some of the Gielow office's drawings are at the Maine Maritime Museum, 243 Washington St., Bath, ME 04530. A number of diesel and steam yachts, like J. P. Morgan's last **Corsair**, were built in Bath in the 1930s after Gielow's death.

An extended obituary was published in the August 1925 issue of *Motor Boating*.

Frederick W. Goeller, Jr.

A talented designer and superb draftsman who was employed for a few years before World War I by *The Rudder*. Among his designs are more than a dozen sail, power, and row boats specifically created for *The Rudder* as how-to-build articles. These range from a 9' skiff named **Pollywog** to the 35' power cruiser **Flying Fish**. Also included in this group is the 12' outboard (and sailing) dinghy that *WoodenBoat* has long offered plans for as the **Goeller Dinghy**. Since, as far as we know, Goeller's original drawings have not survived, his published plans are a viable alternative—although few in number, they are an inspiring body of work. They appear in *The Rudder* beginning in October 1910 and conclude in January 1917.

Henry C. Grebe (1890–1952)

A Chicago-based designer of power cruisers who established his own building yard in 1921.

John L. Hacker (1877–1961)

An intuitive designer of fast and stylish powerboats, based in the Detroit area. A contemporary of Gar Wood, Chris Smith, and Henry Ford, Hacker was a builder, at times, as well as a designer. The Gold Cup hydroplane **El Legarto** and the posh **Belle Isle Bearcat** runabouts are two of his best-known designs. When it came to streamlining, Hacker was at the head of his profession.

Some Hacker drawings are at The Mariners'

Museum, 100 Museum Dr., Newport News, VA 23606, and a number have been published in various periodicals.

The most comprehensive writing about Hacker is by Joseph Gribbins in *Nautical Quarterly* No. 14 (Summer 1981), and there's another revealing piece in the July/August 1996 issue of *Classic Boating* entitled "John Hacker Remembered: A conversation with Tom Flood." A comprehensive article written by Walter Brennan appeared in the December 1959 issue of *Motor Boating*.

Hand, William H., Jr. (1875–1946)

A prolific designer with an exceptionally good eye for handsome boats. Hand's career began around 1900 with small sailboats, but he soon shifted to V-bottomed powerboats. They were his specialty until after World War I when he directed his talent to seakindly schooners. Later, during the 1930s, motorsailers became his passion. Hand's office was in Fairhaven, Massachusetts.

Hand's surviving drawings are at Hart Nautical Collections, MIT Museum, 265 Massachusetts Avenue, Cambridge, MA 02139.

A two-part article on William Hand, published in *WoodenBoat* Nos. 28 and 29 (May/June & July/August 1979), pretty well cover this designer's career, although there's more good material in Waldo Howland's book *A Life in Boats: The Years Before the War*, published by Mystic Seaport in 1984. For a rundown on Hand's drawings, refer to Kurt Hasselbalch's *Guide to Davis-Hand Collection*, published by MIT in 1998.

John G. Hanna (1891–1948)

A Florida-based designer of cruising craft, best remembered for his double-ended **Tahiti** ketch and her larger steel sister, the **Carol** ketch. An opinionated and prolific writer, Hanna for years contributed to boating magazines. His designs often appeared as how-to-build articles for *Mechanix Illustrated* and *How to Build 20 Boats* in its various editions.

After Hanna's death, The Seven Seas Press published a number of his designs, and Seven Seas' Steve Doherty eventually wrote a book about this designer entitled *A Ketch Called* **Tahiti**: *John G. Hanna and His Yacht Designs,* published by International Marine in 1987.

Hanna's drawings are at Calvert Marine Museum, P.O. Box 97, Solomons, MD 20688.

L. Francis Herreshoff (1890–1972)

An innovative designer of racing and cruising boats, Herreshoff contributed to the sport in equal measure through his prolific writings. The striking 72′ ketch **Ticonderoga** may be his most familiar and admired design. Many amateur builders made use of the how-to-build designs created expressly for and published by *The Rudder* in the 1940s and '50s. Among the most successful were the H-28

ketch and the double-ended, ketch-rigged **Rozinante** canoe yawl.

All of Herreshoff's drawings and files are at Mystic Seaport, Greenmanville Avenue, Mystic, CT 06355.

Although LFH's writings are too numerous to list here, his major works are *The Common Sense of Yacht Design,* published in 1946 & 1948 by *The Rudder; Sensible Cruising Designs,* published in 1973 by International Marine; *The Compleat Cruiser,* published in 1963 by Sheridan House; and the biography of his father entitled *Captain Nat Herreshoff, The Wizard of Bristol,* published in 1953 by Sheridan House. A complete list of plans and several of his designs are contained in the book *Boat Plans at Mystic Seaport* by Anne and Maynard Bray, published by Mystic Seaport in 2000.

Frederic D. Lawley (1878–1953)

An MIT-educated son of George F. Lawley, Fred Lawley worked at first as house designer for the Geo. F. Lawley & Son yard in Neponset, Massachusetts, then established his own yard in nearby Quincy.

Some Lawley drawings are at Hart Nautical Collections, MIT Museum, 265 Massachusetts Avenue, Cambridge, MA 02139. More are at Mystic Seaport, Greenmanville Avenue, Mystic, CT 06355.

For historical information on the Lawleys, see *The Archives of the Lawley Boat Owners Association* (3rd edition), available from the Association at P.O. Box 242, Gloucester, MA 01931-0242.

Lee & Brinton

Harold Lee was the firm's chief designer, having been educated at Yale University's Sheffield Scientific School and Cornell University where he majored in naval architecture. He and his partner F. S. Brinton moved from the East Coast and set up their design office in Seattle around 1906. Lee & Brinton's specialty was designing powerboats for Puget Sound cruising.

Numerous Lee & Brinton designs appeared in *Pacific Motor Boat* over the years, but it appears that the firm's drawings have not survived.

A brief article about Harold Lee was published in the April 1911 issue of *Motor Boating*.

Frederick K. Lord (1878–1968)

New York-based designer of fast powerboats as well as the occasional sailing craft. His V-bottomed planing raceboats and runabouts were among the best. Remembered as designer of the Rosenfeld chase boat **Foto**.

Many of Lord's drawings are at Mystic Seaport, Greenmanville Avenue, Mystic, CT 06355.

Alfred E. Luders, Sr. (1880–1964)

Educated at what is now Webb Institute and the University of Glasgow in Scotland, Luders worked for several New York designers before establishing the Luders Marine Construction Co. in 1908.

He designed power craft nearly exclusively, the lovely gaff-rigged sloop **Dyon** shown in the sloop chapter being almost the single exception. His yard got to build nearly all he designed. He was succeeded by his son, A. E. Luders, Jr., who continued with the yard through the mid-1960s, building the **America**'s Cup defender **Weatherly** there to a Rhodes design and later **American Eagle**, which Luders Jr. designed himself.

The entire Luders drawing collection perished in a fire that leveled the yard.

Some Luders records and photos are at Mystic Seaport, Greenmanville Avenue, Mystic, CT 06355.

Charles D. Mower (1875–1942)

A prolific designer with a good eye for form and proportion, Mower designed all types of craft, both power and sail, without specializing in any particular one. He apprenticed with Arthur Binney and B. B. Crowninshield. He worked as a designing editor for *The Rudder* in its early years, and while there designed several how-to-build craft for amateur construction as well as collaborating with editor Thomas Fleming Day in the design of **Sea Bird**, the 27' centerboard yawl in which Day sailed across the Atlantic. He later prepared how-to-build designs for *Motor Boating*. Based in New York for most of his career, Mower was briefly in partnership with Thomas D. Bowes under the name Bowes & Mower. He is remembered for his winning R-class sloops **Ardelle** and **Ardette**, and for designing several other winners under both the Universal and International measurement rules.

Some Mower drawings are at Mystic Seaport, Greenmanville Avenue, Mystic, CT 06355.

The career of this gifted and prolific designer has never been given much attention in print. There is a brief obituary in the February 1942 issue of *The Rudder* and a feature article about Mower in the February 1910 issue of *Motor Boating*. The May 1942 issue of *Yachting* includes a writeup on a few of C. D. Mower's designs.

Ralph M. Munroe (1851–1933)

An early settler in the Miami area of Florida, Commodore Munroe developed shallow and seaworthy sailing yachts for local use by himself and friends. The best-remembered Munroe designs are the sharpie **Egret**, the ketch **Presto**, and the yawl **Micco**. Proas intrigued him during the last half of his life, and he experimented with some small ones.

Most of Munroe's drawings were lost in the 1926 Miami hurricane.

Much has been written by and about Commodore Munroe, the best being *The Commodore's Story* by Munroe himself and published by the Historical Association of Southern Florida in 1985, and *The Good Little Ship* by Vincent Gilpin, published by Sutter House in 1975. There is a fine article in *Nautical Quarterly* No. 45 (Spring 1989) by Steve Henkel as well.

K. Aage Nielsen (1904–1984)

Nielsen began designing in his native Denmark, but while still a young man was hired by John G. Alden where he worked until about 1932. Briefly associated with his friend Murray Peterson, he worked one winter for L. Francis Herreshoff, then became the solitary designer for the Boston office of Sparkman & Stephens where he created a number of designs credited to that firm. He went into business for himself in the Boston area after World War II and became respected for his keel-and-centerboard racing/cruising yachts, mostly yawls, of unusual speed and beauty. He drew all the plans and handled all correspondence himself in this one-man office. Nielsen is best remembered for **Holger Danske**, the heavy, double-ended cruising ketch that won the 1980 Bermuda Race.

All of Nielsen's drawings and files are at the Peabody Essex Museum, East India Square, Salem, MA 01970.

The best biography to date is an obituary written by John Wilson, one of Nielsen's clients, that was published in *Cruising Club News*, January 1985. There is also a piece entitled "'Good Enough' is Not a Sufficient Goal: Aage Nielsen's Double-enders" in *WoodenBoat* No. 133 (Nov/Dec 1996). Steve Corkery and Maynard Bray are writing a book about Nielsen's career and boat designs.

Murray G. Peterson (1908–1974)

A perfectionist who loved traditional detail, Peterson specialized in salty-looking cruising boats, primarily sail, that include the well-loved "Peterson coasting schooners." He began with John G. Alden, but went on his own in the mid-1930s when the Alden office was reduced in size due to the Depression. He remained friendly and loosely associated with Aage Nielsen, and these two talents subsequently collaborated on a few designs, most notably the Danish-type, double-ended ketch **Lille Dansker**, and the keel-centerboard schooner **Defiance**. He is best remembered for his Coaster designs.

All of Peterson's drawings are with his son William N. Peterson, who carries on designing under the name Murray G. Peterson Associates, Inc. HC 64 Box 700, South Bristol, ME 04568.

A major feature on this talented designer has yet to be written, but the obituary by his friend John F. Leavitt in issue No. 1 of *The WoodenBoat* (Sept/Oct 1974) is the best to date.

Purdy Boat Co.

Both Purdy brothers, Ned and Gil, got lots of good experience working at Consolidated Shipbuilding where Ned had been shop foreman and Gil the chief designer. In 1915, Consolidated client Carl Fisher wooed them away and set them up in Indianapolis, Miami, Detroit, and, finally, in Port Washington on Long Island. Gil (1863–1946) was the designer and created raceboats as well as large motoryachts like the 150' steel-hulled **Shadow K** for Fisher and her near sister **Vara** for Harold Vanderbilt. The Purdy boat best remembered, however, is **Aphrodite**, the sleek, 74′ round-sterned commuter built for John Hay Whitney and which is still going strong.

Most of the drawings have been destroyed.

A comprehensive article about the Purdys, written by Ginger Martus and Alan Dinn, was published in *WoodenBoat* No. 126 (September/October 1995).

Philip L. Rhodes (1895–1974)

An MIT-educated designer with one of the finest eyes for form and beauty in the business. His drafting was of the highest order as well, and Rhodes's drawings are always a pleasure to look at and easy to understand. He may be best known for the 12-Meter sloop **Weatherly**, which defended the **America**'s Cup in 1962, but many, many noteworthy designs came from the Rhodes office. His specialty was sailing yachts of the racing/cruising variety, but there were Rhodes designs of other types, large and small, with equal merit. For over a dozen years, beginning in 1934, he was chief designer for Cox & Stevens, taking over the firm and giving it his own name in 1947.

All the Cox & Stevens and Philip L. Rhodes drawings are at Mystic Seaport, Greenmanville Avenue, Mystic, CT 06355.

The best source of information is the book by Richard Henderson entitled *Philip L. Rhodes and His Yacht Designs*, published by International Marine in 1981.

Gilbert (Gil) M. Smith (1843–1930)

A Long Island designer-builder located in Patchogue on Great South Bay where the water is sheltered but shallow. Smith specialized in sleek, fast catboats with varnished decks and big rigs for recreational sailing.

Because Smith designed by making wooden half models instead of drawing lines on paper, few plans ever existed.

Two articles, both published in 1966, tell the Smith story. The first was written by W. H. DeFontaine and was in the March issue of *Yachting*, while the second, by Paul Bigelow, appeared in the June issue of *Long Island Forum*.

Sparkman & Stephens

Winning races with the sailing yachts it created was this firm's obsession from the beginning, just as it was for the genius who propelled it to the top spot among yacht designers. That man is Olin J. Stephens II, who has been behind the design of more winning sailing yachts than anyone in the U.S. Small boats and power yachts were designed there as well, and during the wars the S&S team produced plans for small and medium-sized government craft. S&S 12-Meter sloops, beginning with **Columbia** in 1958, successfully defended the **America**'s Cup six times. The ocean racing yawls

Dorade and **Stormy Weather**, and the 19′ Lightning-class sloops are among S&S's best remembered designs.

S&S drawings are in the process of being donated to Mystic Seaport, and the pre-World War II plans are already there. Others are at the S&S office in New York (529 Fifth Ave., NY, NY 10017).

Three books have been written about S&S, the latest and by far the best being Olin Stephens's autobiography entitled *All This and Sailing Too*, published in 1999 by Mystic Seaport. Others are *You Are First* by Francis S. Kinney, published by Dodd Mead & Co. in 1978, and *The Best of the Best*, by Kinney and Bourne, and published by W. W. Norton in 1996. There is also a comprehensive article in *Professional BoatBuilder* No. 60 (August/September 1999).

Francis Sweisguth (1882–1970)

A New York-based designer who designed the Star-class sloops while working for William Gardner. He was later in partnership with the firm of Ford, Payne & Sweisguth.

Drawings for the **Star** as well as other Sweisguth designs are at Mystic Seaport, Greenmanville Avenue, Mystic, CT 06355.

A short obituary appeared in the August 1970 issue of *Yachting*.

Winthrop L. Warner (1900–1987)

A designer primarily of cruising sailboats, but powerboats, commercial draggers, and a car ferry are sprinkled into his work. He was educated at MIT and worked for Alden, Hand, and briefly for Rhodes before starting his own design business in 1931. The Cambridge Cadet and the Warner 33 are two of his best-remembered designs. Warner's designs were frequently published in the design sections of both *The Rudder* and *Yachting*.

All of Warner's drawings and files are at Mystic Seaport, Greenmanville Avenue, Mystic, CT 06355.

The best writeup on Warner appeared in *WoodenBoat* No. 75 (March/April 1987), written by Kathleen Grobe. Additional material is contained in the book *Boat Plans at Mystic Seaport*, by Anne and Maynard Bray, published by Mystic Seaport in 2000.

J. Murray Watts (1879–1950)

A Philadelphia-based designer of both commercial and pleasure craft whose designs were published with regularity in boating magazines. Watts was educated in naval architecture at Yale's Scientific School, after which he joined the firm of Swasey, Raymond & Page. He was briefly in partnership with Thomas Bowes.

Some of the Watts drawings are at Mystic Seaport, Greenmanville Avenue, Mystic, CT 06355.

John H. Wells (1879–1962)

Educated at Cornell University, Wells worked at Elco, Matthews Boat Co., and for Henry Gielow before setting up under his own name. John Wells's designs first appeared in *Motor Boating* in 1913. His specialty was large motoryachts. His business was absorbed by the J. J. Henry Co. in 1956.

Some of Wells's drawings are at Mystic Seaport, Greenmanville Avenue, Mystic, CT 06355.

Fenwick C. Williams (1901–1992)
A Massachusetts-based designer of small, salty-looking sailboats, especially catboats. Worked at the Alden office and briefly as a partner with Murray Peterson before becoming an independent designer. Drew plans for Ray Hunt's 12-Meter **Easterner** and for the many modifications of the Concordia yawls. Williams's own designs often were based on traditional sailing workboats, and with his meticulous drafting, his drawings are works of art.

Drawings are with Bill Peterson (Murray G. Peterson Associates, HC 64 Box 700, South Bristol, ME 04568) and at Peabody Essex Museum, East India Square, Salem, MA 01970..

A fine article outlining Williams's life, written by Bill Peterson and Fred Bauer, was published in *WoodenBoat* No. 151 (November/December 1999). Waldo Howland's book *A Life in Boats: The Concordia Years*, published by Mystic Seaport in 1988, contains additional information. Williams also wrote extensively for The Catboat Association's *Bulletin. The Catboat Book*, edited by John Leavens and published by International Marine in 1973, has a chapter by Williams entitled "Catboat Design."

Ralph E. Winslow (1886–1957)
The Massachusetts-based Winslow started out designing powerboats and first worked for Small Bros.; William Hand; Swasey, Raymond & Page; Herreshoff Mfg. Co.; and Eldredge-McInnis before permanently setting up under his own name in 1931. From then on he designed mostly cruising sailboats on speculation, many of whose plans were published in *The Rudder* and *Yachting*.

Winslow's drawings are at Mystic Seaport, Greenmanville Avenue, Mystic, CT 06355, and quite a number of the World War I-era Herreshoff Mfg. Co. drawings (preserved at MIT) show the unmistakable Winslow touch.

The best published information on Winslow was written by Weston Farmer in his book *From My Old Boat Shop*, published by International Marine in 1996.